OFFICERS & SOLDIERS

FRENCH DRAGOONS

1750-1792

Volume II
From the Seven Years War to the French Revolution

Véronique and **Ludovic LETRUN**
Translated from the French by Jennifer Meyniel

Histoire & Collections

THE KING DRAGOONS
1750-1792

In this second half of the 18th century, military tactics changed, going from static siege tactics to rapid manoeuvres, giving the cavalry a predominant role again on the field of battle.

During the Age of Enlightenment, Louis XV and his grandson Louis XVI, peaceful monarchs who were little attracted to warfare, had to find gifted ministers and men to make up for the kingdom's lack of preparedness, against the warmongering Prussian, Austrian and English forces.

Despite its setbacks and the loss of its colonies, France remained the most influential and populated country in Europe. In view of its important geopolitical position, France's army had to be modernised without unsettling the comfort of its persisting internal feudality.

Despite some reticence, two renowned men, Choiseul in 1762 and Saint-Germain in 1775 with experience from abroad created a new army.

The changes in uniform, organisation and tactics of the Dragoon regiments evolved over three periods. The main corps gradually joined with the cavalry, becoming a key element in the new strategy of movement. The first period, included ordinances from 1750 and 1757, and mainly improved the troop's comfort. The second period of change, under the ordinances from 1762 and 1767 reorganised and unified the corps. Finally the last period under the ordinances from 1776, 1779 and 1786 provided the republic with the most modern corps and army in the world.

ORDINANCE FROM MAY 1ST 1750

Despite its glorious stature following the War of Austrian succession in 1748, the Royal Army saw its numbers dramatically reduced to relieve the Kingdom's finances. This was the price paid following a peace treaty that was signed, and which only benefitted the King of Prussia. The Dragoons, mounted infantry, also suffered unjust restrictive measures from September 1st 1748. The mixed corps was made up of 16 regiments, each one made up of 12 companies of 44 Dragoons, 24 mounted and 20 infantry, totalling 528 men, 288 mounted and 240 infantry per regiment, and 8448 men in the entire army.

A regiment only had 4 foot companies grouped in a demi-battalion and 8 mounted companies grouped in two squadrons. Each foot company included a senior captain, a lieutenant, a second lieutenant, 3 sergeants, 4 corporals, 4 *anspessades*, 1 drummer and 60 Dragoons.

The following October, each regiment had only 8 squadrons from a company made up 30 men on horseback and 4 infantry companies.

Despite the prevailing restrictions, the King ordained by order on May 1st 1750, the renewal of uniforms, equipment and weapons for the Dragoons. The Prussian model was chosen for this second text, following the first of its kind in 1733. To avoid non regulatory uses, the text was placed under the control of the Colonel General of the Dragoons, the Duke of Coigny and the *Mestre de camp general* of the Dragoons, the Duke of Chevreuse. Reforms had to be meticulously overseen by leaders during future amendments.

Uniforms

The *justaucorps* for the Dragoons, brigadier generals, anspessades and *carabiniers* were made from Lodève or Berry serge in blue and various shades of red, lined with serge from Aumale or caddis. The facings, the cuffs of the imitation pockets and the back opening all had three white buttonholes. The front of the outfit was decorated up to the pockets on each side, white buttonholes placed at an equal distance, or in pairs or in threes depending on the regiment. Useful pockets were hidden in the pleats at the back of the outfit between the lining and the serge. A woollen epaulette with the colours of the regimental livery was buttoned to the left shoulder to keep the *giberne*'s strap in place.

The tailed jacket was made from the same material as the *justacorps*, lined with white linen and decorated to the bottom with the same white buttonholes. It only fastened up to the pocket cuffs decorated with three buttonholes.

The tunic's sleeves were open and were decorated with three small buttonholes.

The bonnet worn off duty or during parades was replaced for all other occasions by the hat. The bonnet had turn backs in the same colour as the facings with the livery and flame edged in the same colour as the outfit's main colour.

The flame was edged in white with the tip decorated with a white crest and the livery. The black woollen hat had a silver stripe and was decorated with a cockade made from black taffeta, fixed in place by a braid of black horsehair. During battle

Colonel-Général Dragons — 1750-1757

In accordance with the ordinance 1750, Dragoon with a red outfit, blue facings and lining, blue jacket with white edges, white sabre cord and epaulettes, white buttonholes, blue equipage edged with white and the Colonel-Général's decorations.

Dragoon, in accordance with the ordinance 1757, identical to the previous regulation except for the *ceinturon* belt and the bayonet.

From 1754 to 1771, the drummers wore the unknown livery of the House of Luynes.

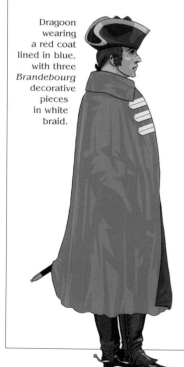

Dragoon wearing a red coat lined in blue, with three *Brandebourg* decorative pieces in white braid.

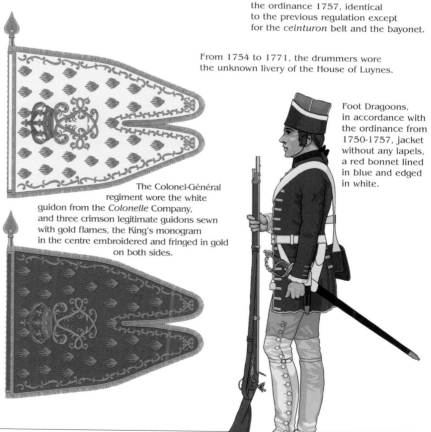

The Colonel-Général regiment wore the white guidon from the *Colonelle* Company, and three crimson legitimate guidons sewn with gold flames, the King's monogram in the centre embroidered and fringed in gold on both sides.

Foot Dragoons, in accordance with the ordinance from 1750-1757, jacket without any lapels, a red bonnet lined in blue and edged in white.

an iron skull cap was put on over the troop's headpieces or a leather skull cap was worn by the officers.

The leather culottes were fastened by five or six wooden buttons on which white woollen cuffs were placed to limit the rubbing from the boots.

The boots were made from calf leather, oiled to make them more supple, attached all the way up at the side with leather buckles. Iron spurs were fixed permanently.

The gaiters regulatory since 1736 were worn during foot service. They were made from white linen, lined above and below the foot, they fastened at the side with a series of either bone or leather buttons, and they were held in place by garters under the knees.

The sleeveless coat with the turned down collar was made from Lodève serge and was the same colour as the outfit's main shade. It was lined at the front by two bands of caddis or serge in the same colour as the facings. The upper chest was decorated on each side with three decorative pieces or *brandebourgs* with the livery's stripe. The coat's tails were gathered up to prevent them from obstructing the march during foot parades. The sheep skin gloves were only worn during parades and during battle.

The buffalo-hide *ceinturon* belt was stitched in white and fastened with a brass buckle, there was a double holder for a sword and a bayonet *(page 9)* With the introduction of the new bayonet and the 1754 model Dragoons rifle, a new and fuller equipped ceinturon belt was supplied with two holders sewn on with brass buckles large and long enough to fit the sword and the bayonet *(page 9)*.

The *giberne*, still known as the cartridge belt or the *demi-giberne* was made from Russian hide with a wooden box containing thirty cartridges. The strap sewn to the giberne was made from boiled buffalo hide, it had a crosspiece that fastened at the chest with a brass buckle *(page 9)*.

The haversack, also used for sleeping purposes, it was made from hemp, in a rectangular piece measuring 130 cm by 80 cm, it was supplied with a leather strap that fastened with a copper buckle. The ordinance of February 17th 1753, supplied a new haversack with two straps to relieve the backs of Dragoons on foot service (picture N°4). Under the same ordinance, 5 cloth tents were supplied for 40 foot soldiers.

Weapons

The Dragoons were armed with 1750 model cavalry sabres with a narrow frame and double branches, a slightly curbed back blade that were no longer than 90 cm. The wooden scabbard was covered with animal skin and decorated with a cap and a brass tip. The woollen cord was the same colour as the epaulette. There was a large variety of this kind of weapon, produced over a long period of time by numerous manufacturers. Since 1745 the Aubigné regiment was the first and only regiment to acquire the iron-framed sabre with demi-basket protection.

In 1750, the Dragoons were still armed with the 1733 infantry model rifle, adapted for their own use. 6 000 rifles were produced measuring 153 cm, decorated with brass and a Russian leather strap which was fastened by two rings on the left hand side. The bayonet, specific to the Dragoons had a flat blade measuring 32.5 cm.

Only 3 500 rifles were produced of the new 1754 model. It was used in addition to the model from 1733, it didn't completely replace it. It was 5 cm shorter than the infantry rifle, and also lighter and easier to handle. It was characterised by its iron double-banded grenadier with its red Russian leather strap under the barrel. They also used the infantry split socket bayonet that adjusted to the pin fixed to the right of the barrel.

Finally each Dragoon was armed with a cavalry 1733 model pistol, measuring 48.6 cm, and weighing 1,230 kg. It was kept in the holder on the left hand side of the saddle, or hooked to their *ceinturon* belts for the foot soldiers.

Equipage and horse tack

The saddlecloth, the calotte and *bavette* chaperon were made from Lodève or Berry serge, in blue or red, edged with the livery of the colonels and lined with linen.

Although the horse tack was identical, it was smaller than that of the cavalry, with the seat and flaps, halter and bridle headgear in darkened leather but without any muzzle. The font was made from Russian leather, the bit had straight branches and brass *bossettes*. There were two rings on the pommel fixed with iron, suspending the sheath and a strap for the rifle's barrel. There was also a ring on the sheath for the tent pegs. The horse had to carry heavy loads of 70 kg in addition to the cavalier. The ordinance dated May 1st 1750, provided 20 tools for each of the foot or mounted companies, 4 shovels, 4 pick axes, 4 machetes and 8 large axes *(page 9)*.

Bas-officiers (sub-officers or NCOs)

The *Maréchal-des-logis* wore quite thick cloth from Romorantin, they carried the troop's sabre with a straight blade and an equipage edged with silver stripe, 27 mm wide.

The sergeants wore the same outfit, the same sabre as the Maréchal-des-logis but with the troop's equipage.

The carabiner and the anspessades wore outfits with silver stripes with silk measuring 23 mm wide on the facings. The caporal and the brigadier had three buttonholes on their facings braided with silver and silk, measuring 23 mm wide.

Mestre-de-camp-général dragons, 2ᵉ régiment

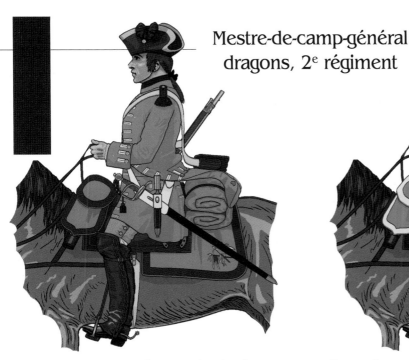

In accordance with the ordinance from 1750, in red outfit, facings linings and jacket, white buttonholes, black sabre cord and epaulettes, the red bonnet was edged in black, red equipage embroidered in black and probably the trophies from the Mestre-de-Camp Général.

Dragoon, in accordance with the ordinance from 1757, with braiding, facings, lining, sabre cord and epaulette in white.

The drummers wore the unknown livery of the House of Coigny.

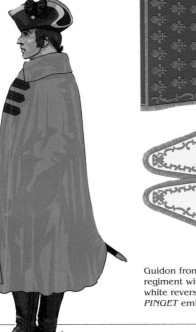

Dragoon wearing red coat, with three black braid decorations in 1750 (later white lining and decorative pieces in 1757).

Guidon from the Mestre-de-Camp Général regiment with blue obverse with *fleur de lis*, white reverse bearing the motto *VICTORIA PINGET* embroidered and fringed in gold.

Foot Dragoon in accordance with the ordinance from 1757, with lapels on the red jacket or a small white shoulder strap.

7

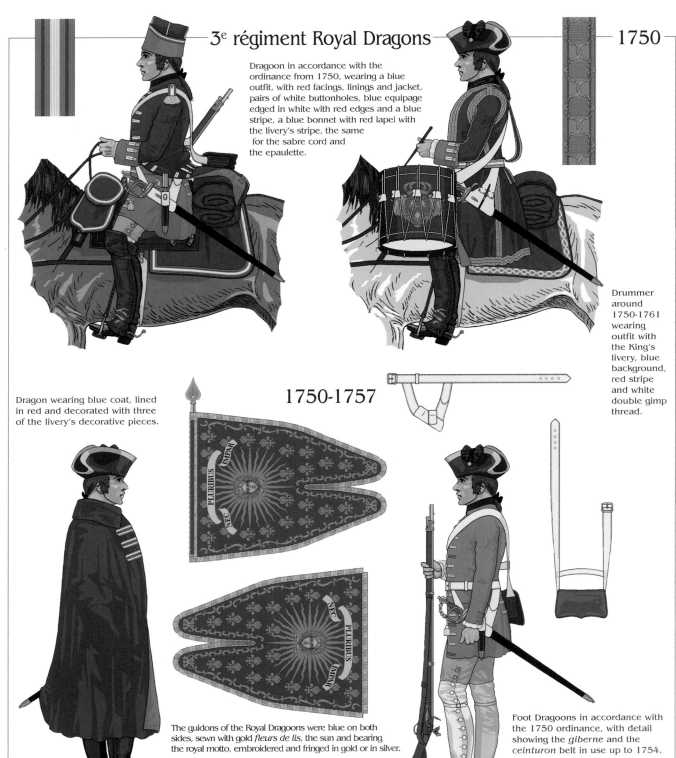

3ᵉ régiment Royal Dragons

1750

Dragoon in accordance with the ordinance from 1750, wearing a blue outfit, with red facings, linings and jacket, pairs of white buttonholes, blue equipage edged in white with red edges and a blue stripe, a blue bonnet with red lapel with the livery's stripe, the same for the sabre cord and the epaulette.

Drummer around 1750-1761 wearing outfit with the King's livery, blue background, red stripe and white double gimp thread.

1750-1757

Dragon wearing blue coat, lined in red and decorated with three of the livery's decorative pieces.

The guidons of the Royal Dragoons were blue on both sides, sewn with gold *fleurs de lis*, the sun and bearing the royal motto, embroidered and fringed in gold or in silver.

Foot Dragoons in accordance with the 1750 ordinance, with detail showing the *giberne* and the *ceinturon* belt in use up to 1754.

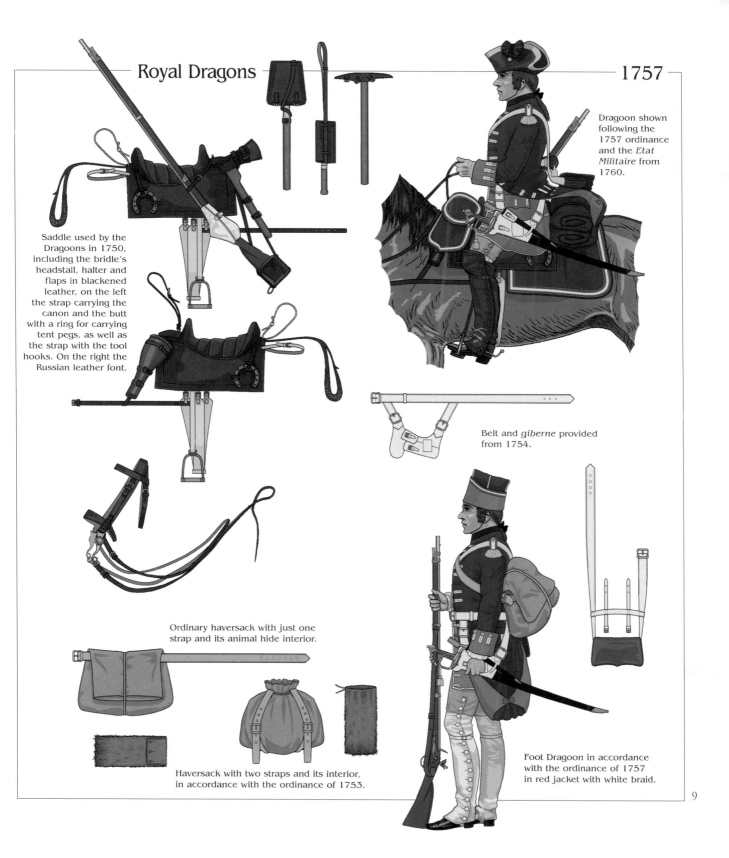

Saddle used by the Dragoons in 1750, including the bridle's headstall, halter and flaps in blackened leather, on the left the strap carrying the canon and the butt with a ring for carrying tent pegs, as well as the strap with the tool hooks. On the right the Russian leather font.

Dragoon shown following the 1757 ordinance and the *Etat Militaire* from 1760.

Belt and *giberne* provided from 1754.

Ordinary haversack with just one strap and its animal hide interior.

Haversack with two straps and its interior, in accordance with the ordinance of 1753.

Foot Dragoon in accordance with the ordinance of 1757 in red jacket with white braid.

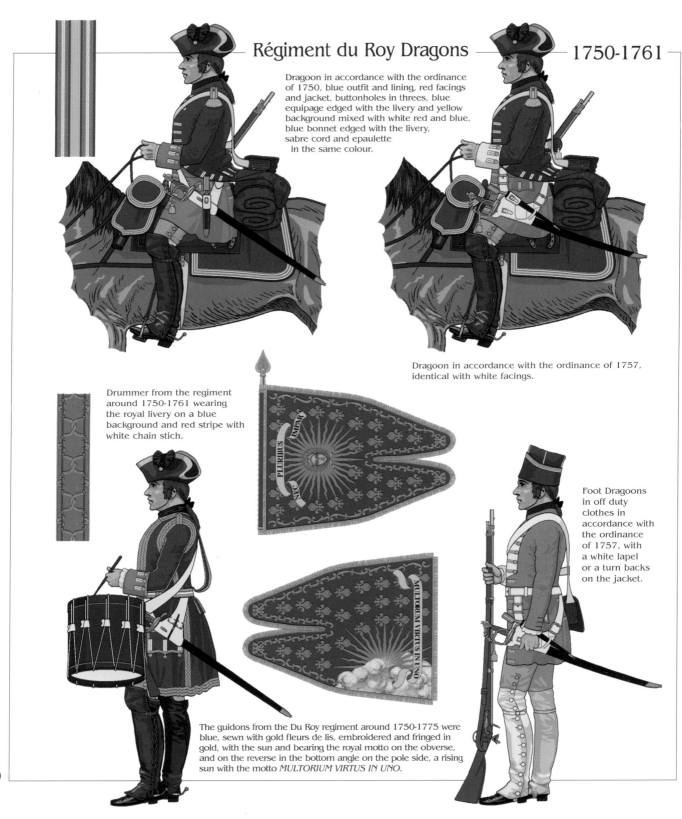

Régiment du Roy Dragons

1750-1761

Dragoon in accordance with the ordinance of 1750, blue outfit and lining, red facings and jacket, buttonholes in threes, blue equipage edged with the livery and yellow background mixed with white red and blue, blue bonnet edged with the livery, sabre cord and epaulette in the same colour.

Dragoon in accordance with the ordinance of 1757, identical with white facings.

Drummer from the regiment around 1750-1761 wearing the royal livery on a blue background and red stripe with white chain stich.

Foot Dragoons in off duty clothes in accordance with the ordinance of 1757, with a white lapel or a turn backs on the jacket.

PLURIBUS IMPAR NEC

MULTORUM VIRTUS IN UNO

The guidons from the Du Roy regiment around 1750-1775 were blue, sewn with gold fleurs de lis, embroidered and fringed in gold, with the sun and bearing the royal motto on the obverse, and on the reverse in the bottom angle on the pole side, a rising sun with the motto *MULTORIUM VIRTUS IN UNO*.

10

La Reine Dragons
5e Régiment

Dragoon in accordance with the 2nd *Carte Militaire* of 1754 and the ordinance of 1757, with buttonholes in threes.

Dragoon in accordance with the ordinance of 1750, red outfit with blue facings, linings and jacket, buttonholes in pairs, red equipage edged with the queen's livery's stripe on a blue background with white chain stich and a red bonnet with blue turn backs with the livery's stripe, sabre cord and epaulette in the colours of the livery.

The drummer from La Reine regiment wore the livery on a red background with blue stripe and white chain stich, the drum was red with fleurs de lis and the Queen's coat of arms.

Foot Dragoon in accordance with the ordinance of 1757, with a red lapel or turn backs on the blue jacket.

The guidons from la Reine from 1725 to 1770 were red, sewn with gold and silver *fleur de lis*, with the sun and bearing the royal motto on the obverse, as well as the coat of arms of the Queen Marie Leczinska on the reverse.

11

The drummers from the royal regiments wore the King's livery, and those from gentleman's regiments wore the colonels' livery. Tabards were fastened by hooks and they didn't have pocket cuffs. The drum was painted in the colours of the regiment and the Arms of the *gentilhomme*, it was smaller than the infantry drum and it was beaten differently. The distinction of drum major wasn't

Officers

The officer wore a uniform similar to the troop's but in the finer Elbeuf cloth, with decorative buttons and buttonholes and on the left shoulder a sliver strap. Officers were armed with a shorter 144 cm rifle, with brass decorative pieces and a bayonet with a flat blade measuring 28.3 cm. The *giberne* was made from boiled buffalo hide and was stitched in white, with a bayonet holder on the strap, which was non-existent on the white *ceinturon* belt. The equipage was made from fine cloth with the colours of the troop, it was edged with a distinctive silver stripe measuring 5.4 cm for captains and 4 cm for lieutenants. There were no official ordinances for officers' horse tack, so a certain amount of fantasy was tolerated. Before 1762, the guidon bearer was chosen from the lieutenants.

The ordinance provided officers from the cavalry and the Dragoons with the "Musketeer" 1750 model sword with a golden brass mount, the fuse had copper filigree and a straight blade measuring 85 cm.

ORDINANCE FROM APRIL 9th 1757

Corps diversity was abolished on August 18th 1755, from which date each regiment was made up of 16 companies of 40 Dragoons and sub-officers, making a total of 640 men for each regiment and 10240 men for the corps all of whom were mounted. However during the Seven Years' war during which most of the regiments were assigned to coastal defence, lack of horses forced four regiments to carry out the "small war" on foot like the infantry, to which the corps was still part. Each regiment had four squadrons, each made up of four companies, with headquarters commanded by a colonel (and not a *Mestre de camp* like in the cavalry), 1 lieutenant general, 1 major, 1 assistant major, 1 deputy assistant major and 1 chaplain. Each company included 1 captain, 1 lieutenant, 1 cornet, 1 *Maréchal-des-logis*, 2 brigadiers, 4 *carabiniers*, 1 quartermaster, 32 Dragoons and 1 drum player.

Outfit

The former ordinance didn't give full satisfaction, so a third order was issued on April 9th 1757, to amend some details in order to better differentiate regiments.

The distribution of distinctive colours on the facings, linings, hearts on the lapels or the saddlecloth and chaperons were partly altered. The buttons were placed above the pocket flaps, jackets decorated with a lapel or a small flap on the left sleeve in the same distinctive colour as the lining. The *giberne* remained the same with the addition of two small straps on the banner's crosspiece to attach the bonnet *(page 9)*.

ORDINANCE FROM DECEMBER 21st 1762

Following the disastrous and ruinous Seven Years' War from 1756 to 1763, Frederic II, the Duke of Choiseul Head of war affairs since 1761, undertook considerable reforms concerning the organisation, tactics and uniforms of the Royal Army. He had undertaken a careful study of Vienna, the Austrian armies and in particular the Prussian armies and he used them as a model. The stakes were high as the aim was to win back the American colonies renounced to England.

On December 21st 1726 an extremely innovative order was released that would influence the organisation of the Dragoons and their uniform. The French style coat made from dark green cloth, favoured by the Marshall of Saxe, was adopted by all of the Dragoon regiments. Moreover, the regiments were only recognizable after the new distribution of distinctive colours on the collars, facings and lapels. The copper helmet which was also inspired from the *Volontaires de Saxe*, became common following the Dragoon's enthusiastic reaction. Choiseul ordered them in 1765 to take off their headgear inside churches. Following the successive ordinances, the Dragoons' outfits became increasingly sophisticated, comfortable and were cut closer to the body. In the ordinance of 1762, all of the 17 regiments were divided into 8 companies, made up of 30 Dragoons and mounted sub officers, 1 captain, 1 lieutenant, 1 second lieutenant and 1 drum player, and 16 foot Dragoons, making a regiment of 368 men, 240 on horseback and 128 on foot, totally 6256 men.

From this point on it was the King who supplied the recruits and the mounts, while the major in charge of administration of the mass was accountable for the balance, feed, outfit and weapons, this displeased the captains who owned the companies, and who saw their responsibilities was withdrawn. The recruitment and training became the same as in the cavalry with training in the riding schools.

On November 25th 1766, the composition of each regiment was altered again, with for each one, 8 companies of 38 Dragoons and mounted sub officers, and of 12 foot Dragoons, totally 400 men, 304 of whom were mounted and 96 of whom were foot soldiers, totally 6800 men for the entire corps.

(Continued on page 24)

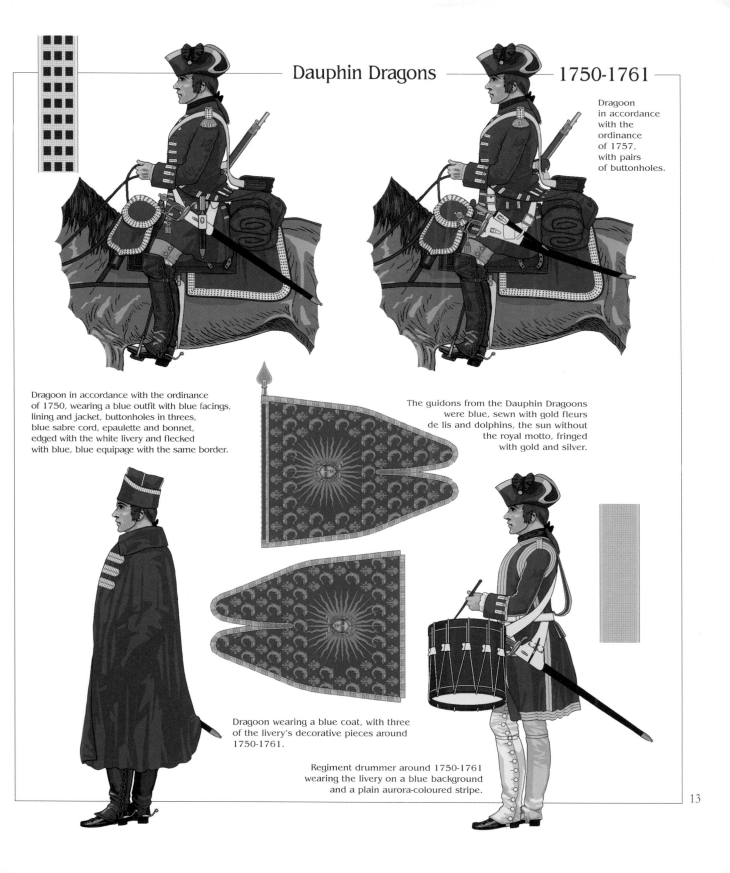

Dauphin Dragons — 1750-1761

Dragoon in accordance with the ordinance of 1757, with pairs of buttonholes.

Dragoon in accordance with the ordinance of 1750, wearing a blue outfit with blue facings, lining and jacket, buttonholes in threes, blue sabre cord, epaulette and bonnet, edged with the white livery and flecked with blue, blue equipage with the same border.

The guidons from the Dauphin Dragoons were blue, sewn with gold fleurs de lis and dolphins, the sun without the royal motto, fringed with gold and silver.

Dragoon wearing a blue coat, with three of the livery's decorative pieces around 1750-1761.

Regiment drummer around 1750-1761 wearing the livery on a blue background and a plain aurora-coloured stripe.

Orléans Dragons

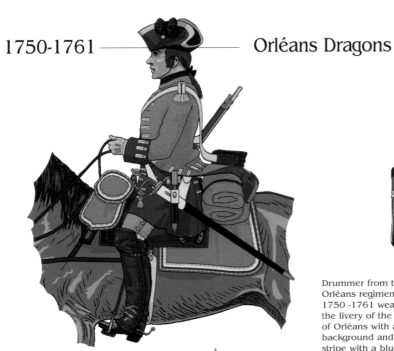

Drummer from the Orléans regiment around 1750 -1761 wearing the livery of the House of Orléans with a red background and white stripe with a blue line running through it and two red chain stiches.

Dragoon in accordance with the ordinance of 1750, wearing a red outfit with blue facings, lining and jacket, white buttonholes in threes, red bonnet with blue lapel bordered with the livery of Orléans stripe, blue sabre cord, epaulette and equipage with the same border.

Dragoon wearing a red coat lined in blue and decorated with three of the livery decorative pieces.

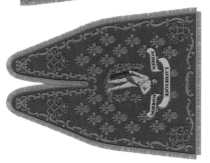

Foot Dragoon in accordance with the ordinance of 1757, with a red outfit, blue facings, lining and jacket, buttonholes in threes, red equipage with the livery's stripe.

The guidons of Orléans were always embroidered, fringed and sewn with fleurs de lis on scarlet silk, with an oval shield of the family of Orléans on the obverse. On the reverse an allegory between two laurel branches, Heracles leaning on his mace, wearing the hide of the Nemean lion with the silver listel bearing the motto *NOMEN LAUDESQUE MANEBUNT*.

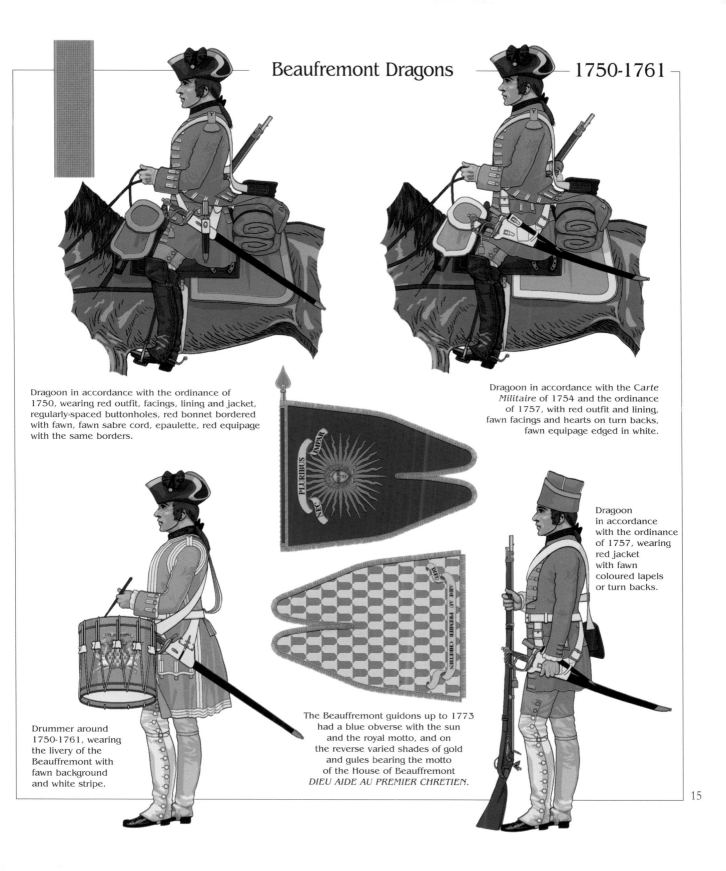

Beaufremont Dragons — 1750-1761

Dragoon in accordance with the ordinance of 1750, wearing red outfit, facings, lining and jacket, regularly-spaced buttonholes, red bonnet bordered with fawn, fawn sabre cord, epaulette, red equipage with the same borders.

Dragoon in accordance with the *Carte Militaire* of 1754 and the ordinance of 1757, with red outfit and lining, fawn facings and hearts on turn backs, fawn equipage edged in white.

Dragoon in accordance with the ordinance of 1757, wearing red jacket with fawn coloured lapels or turn backs.

Drummer around 1750-1761, wearing the livery of the Beauffremont with fawn background and white stripe.

The Beauffremont guidons up to 1773 had a blue obverse with the sun and the royal motto, and on the reverse varied shades of gold and gules bearing the motto of the House of Beauffremont *DIEU AIDE AU PREMIER CHRETIEN.*

Aubigné Dragons

Dragoon in accordance with the ordinance of 1750, red outfit with facings, linings and jacket, regularly-spaced buttonholes, red bonnet bordered with the livery's white stripe and two red *zig zags*, sabre cord and epaulettes from two colours, red equipage edged with the livery.

Dragoon in accordance with the ordinance of 1757, with red outfit and lining, facings and hearts on the turn backs in light green, red equipage bordered with the livery.

Dragoon with red coat, decorated with three of the livery's decorative pieces. The musicians' livery from the House of Aubigné is unknown.

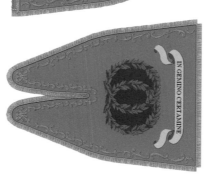

Dragoon in accordance with the ordinance of 1757, wearing red jacket with lapels or turn backs in the same colour as the facings.

The guidons from Aubigné and Choiseul, from 1745 to 1763 were red, embroidered fringed in gold, with the sun and bearing the royal motto on the obverse and on the reverse two natural laurel crowns with the motto *IN GEMINO CERTAMINE.*

16

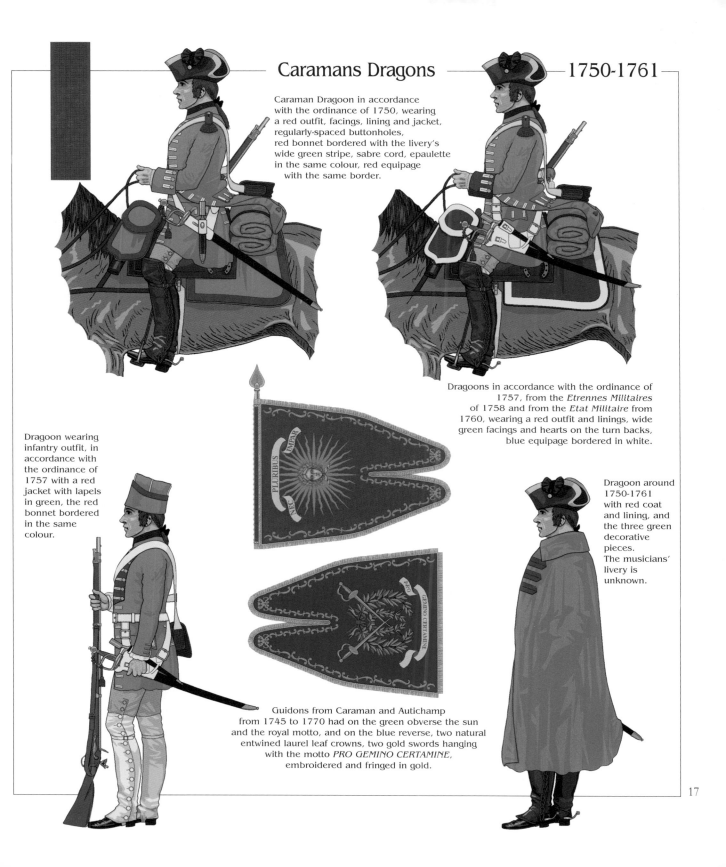

Caraman Dragoon in accordance
with the ordinance of 1750, wearing
a red outfit, facings, lining and jacket,
regularly-spaced buttonholes,
red bonnet bordered with the livery's
wide green stripe, sabre cord, epaulette
in the same colour, red equipage
with the same border.

Dragoons in accordance with the ordinance of
1757, from the *Etrennes Militaires*
of 1758 and from the *Etat Militaire* from
1760, wearing a red outfit and linings, wide
green facings and hearts on the turn backs,
blue equipage bordered in white.

Dragoon wearing
infantry outfit, in
accordance with
the ordinance of
1757 with a red
jacket with lapels
in green, the red
bonnet bordered
in the same
colour.

Dragoon around
1750-1761
with red coat
and lining, and
the three green
decorative
pieces.
The musicians'
livery is
unknown.

Guidons from Caraman and Autichamp
from 1745 to 1770 had on the green obverse the sun
and the royal motto, and on the blue reverse, two natural
entwined laurel leaf crowns, two gold swords hanging
with the motto *PRO GEMINO CERTAMINE*,
embroidered and fringed in gold.

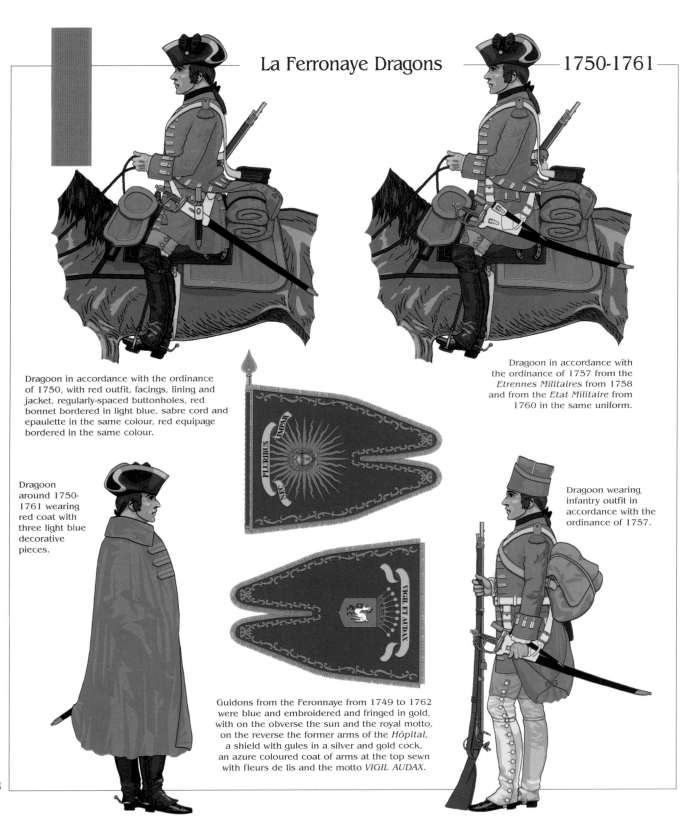

La Ferronaye Dragons — 1750-1761

Dragoon in accordance with the ordinance of 1750, with red outfit, facings, lining and jacket, regularly-spaced buttonholes, red bonnet bordered in light blue, sabre cord and epaulette in the same colour, red equipage bordered in the same colour.

Dragoon in accordance with the ordinance of 1757 from the *Etrennes Militaires* from 1758 and from the *Etat Militaire* from 1760 in the same uniform.

Dragoon around 1750-1761 wearing red coat with three light blue decorative pieces.

Dragoon wearing infantry outfit in accordance with the ordinance of 1757.

Guidons from the Feronnaye from 1749 to 1762 were blue and embroidered and fringed in gold, with on the obverse the sun and the royal motto, on the reverse the former arms of the *Hôpital*, a shield with gules in a silver and gold cock, an azure coloured coat of arms at the top sewn with fleurs de lis and the motto *VIGIL AUDAX*.

Harcourt & Flamarens Dragons

Dragoon from Harcourt, in accordance with the ordinance of 1750, wearing outfit with facings, lining and jacket in red, regularly-spaced buttonholes, red bonnet bordered with yellow and black stripe, sabre cord and epaulette in the same colours, red equipage bordered in the same colours.

Dragoon from Harcourt in accordance with the ordinance of 1757, with black facings and hearts on the turn backs, buttonholes in pairs.

Dragoon in infantry outfit, in accordance with the ordinance of 1757 with red jacket and black lapels.

Drummer wearing the livery of the House of Harcourt, red background with double red and yellow squared stripe.

The guidons from Harcourt from 1728 to 1765 were fringed in gold and silver, crimson obverse with the sun and the royal motto and on the reverse yellow damas with the allegory of a cloud striking a castle with the motto *FULGURE CITTUS*.

PLURIBUS IMPAR NEC

FULGURE CITTUS

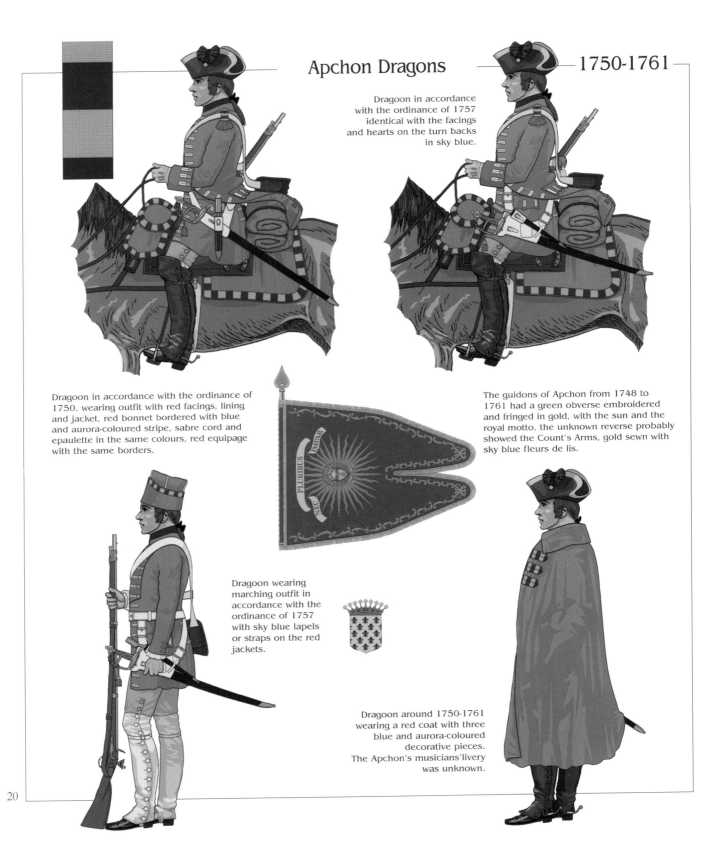

Apchon Dragons

1750-1761

Dragoon in accordance
with the ordinance of 1757
identical with the facings
and hearts on the turn backs
in sky blue.

Dragoon in accordance with the ordinance of
1750, wearing outfit with red facings, lining
and jacket, red bonnet bordered with blue
and aurora-coloured stripe, sabre cord and
epaulette in the same colours, red equipage
with the same borders.

The guidons of Apchon from 1748 to
1761 had a green obverse embroidered
and fringed in gold, with the sun and the
royal motto, the unknown reverse probably
showed the Count's Arms, gold sewn with
sky blue fleurs de lis.

Dragoon wearing
marching outfit in
accordance with the
ordinance of 1757
with sky blue lapels
or straps on the red
jackets.

Dragoon around 1750-1761
wearing a red coat with three
blue and aurora-coloured
decorative pieces.
The Apchon's musicians' livery
was unknown.

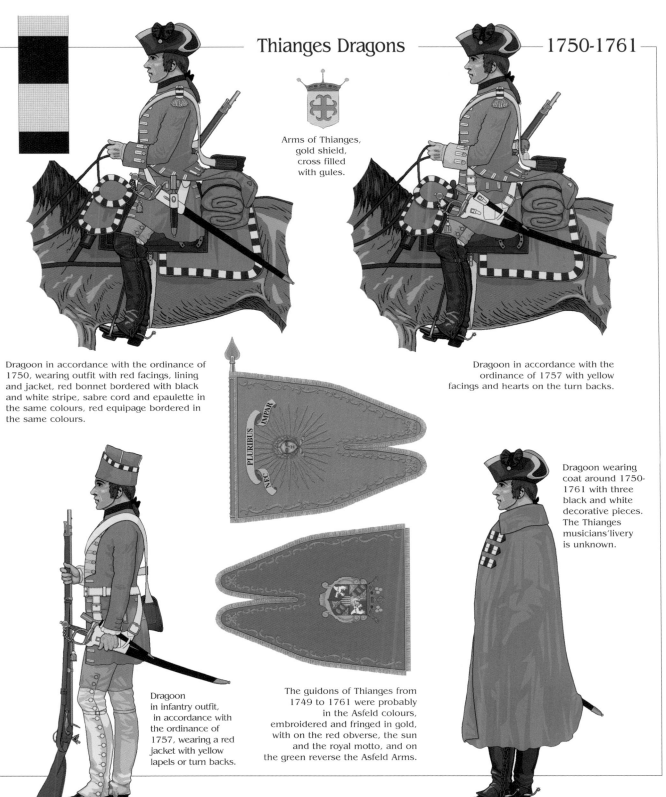

Arms of Thianges,
gold shield,
cross filled
with gules.

Dragoon in accordance with the ordinance of
1750, wearing outfit with red facings, lining
and jacket, red bonnet bordered with black
and white stripe, sabre cord and epaulette in
the same colours, red equipage bordered in
the same colours.

Dragoon in accordance with the
ordinance of 1757 with yellow
facings and hearts on the turn backs.

Dragoon wearing
coat around 1750-
1761 with three
black and white
decorative pieces.
The Thianges
musicians' livery
is unknown.

Dragoon
in infantry outfit,
in accordance with
the ordinance of
1757, wearing a red
jacket with yellow
lapels or turn backs.

The guidons of Thianges from
1749 to 1761 were probably
in the Asfeld colours,
embroidered and fringed in gold,
with on the red obverse, the sun
and the royal motto, and on
the green reverse the Asfeld Arms.

PLURIBUS IMPAR NEC

21

Marbeuf Dragons

Dragoon in accordance with the ordinance of 1750 in outfit with red facings, lining and jacket, red bonnet bordered with white stripe with purple thread, sabre cord and epaulettes in the same colours, red equipage with the same borders.

The Egmont guidons and the Marbeuf guidons from 1744 to 1761, on a crimson background, embroidered and fringed in gold, on the obverse the sun and the royal devise and probably the arms or an allegory on the reverse side.

Dragoon in accordance with the ordinance of 1757, identical with buttonholes in threes. The coat was fully red with three decorative stripes with the livery. The drummers' livery is unknown.

Carabinier from the Marbeuf regiment, wearing marching outfit in accordance with the ordinance of 1757, to distinguish himself his outfit was edged with facings, and silver silk stripe. The jacket seems to be decorated with a sleeve cuff in the distinctive colour.

Arms of the Count of Egmont (on the left) and of the Marquis of Marquis (on the right).

Officer from the Marbeuf regiment in accordance with the ordinance of 1750, wearing the same coat as the troop but made from a better quality serge, with a silver strap on the left.

Languedoc Dragons

Dragoon in accordance with the ordinance of 1750, in outfit, blue lining and jacket, pairs of buttonholes, red facings, pockets and facings decorated with four buttonholes, red bonnet bordered with blue and white stripe, sabre cord and epaulette in the same colours, red equipage with the same border.

Dragoon from the Languedoc regiment in accordance with the ordinance of 1757, identical with the hearts of the red turn backs.

Dragoons in infantry outfit in accordance with the ordinance of 1757, with lapels or turn backs in red. The coat is fully in blue with three decorative pieces of white and blue braid.

Drummer from the Languedoc regiment wearing the King's livery from 1750 to 1761.

The guidons from the Languedoc regiment were embroidered and fringed with gold, with a royal blue obverse sewn with fleur de lis , the sun and bearing the royal motto, and the yellow reverse with the Arms of Languedoc, with gules forming the cross *clechée* , hollowed and covered in gold.

23

Habiliments

The 1762 order assigned the new "French–style" outfit for *Maréchaux-des-logis*, quartermasters, brigadiers, supplementary staff and Dragoons, it was made from Lodève or Barry cloth, lined in serge from Aumale or green caddis from Saxe. The facings'turn backs were decorated with three or four large buttons, the lapels had six or seven small buttons spread out depending on the regiment. There were four large buttons under the lapels on the right to fasten the outfit across the stomach. The pewter buttons were two different sizes with circular knots and gadrooning, stamped with the regimental number or the princes'coat of arms. Only the first two regiments had aurora coloured buttonholes with brass buttons. All of the regiments had upturned collars held in place under the lapels by the top buttons. The imitation pockets became a secondary distinction for each regiment that wore them lengthwise, sideways, single or double. The pockets used for the outfit were hidden in the side pleats of the tailbacks, between the lining and the cloth. The outfit had a woollen fringed shoulder lapel on the left and on the right an aiguillette with the livery's colours or from silk for the *Maréchaux-des-logis*.

Distinctive colours were allocated as follows:
— *Colonel General*, crimson lapels, facings and collar
— *Mestre-de-Camp* red lapels, facings and collars
— *Royal*, red lapels, facings and collar
— *Du Roy* dark pink lapels, facings and collar
— *La Reine* purple lapels, facings and collar
— *Dauphin* purple lapels and facings and green collar
— *Orléans* red lapels and collar with green facings
— *Beauffremont* green collar and buck coloured lapels
— *Choiseul* lemon yellow lapels and facings and collar
— *Autichamp* dark pink lapels and collar, with green facings
— *Chabot* buck coloured lapels, facings and collar
— *Coigny* black lapels, facings and collar
— *Nicolaï* aurora lapels, facings and collar
— *Chapt* yellow lapels and collar with green facings
— *Chabrillan* aurora lapels and facings with green collar
— *Languedoc* white lapels and collar with green facings
— *Schomberg* scarlet lapels, facings and collar.

The jacket was made from fawn cloth lined with caddis or white serge, it fastened at the front by small white buttons with matelote sleeves. It had two imitation pockets and a shoulder strap in the distinctive colour.

The helmet inspired by the Schomberg Dragoons had a copper dome with a crest with the head of Medusa at the front decorated with a curly black mane, or a white mane for the *Colonelle* company from the first regiment. The slightly stiff leather band was covered in sealskin, it was fixed around the head with a buckle at the rear. Each side of the band was stamped a copper rosette, with, on the left, a bow from white ribbon (a cockade) and a white feather for full dress. When necessary a leather visor was attached as well as hooks for a leather chinstrap. The hair was powdered and attached in a ponytail at the nape.

The culottes modelled on the "Bavarian–style" were made from buckskin or sheepskin; they were fastened with buttons with white woollen cuffs to protect from the rubbing of the boots.

The sleeveless coat was made from Lodève cloth, it was grey-white with blue quilting, and it had a large upturned collar and an adjustable hood to protect the helmet. It fastened by hooks with three *Brandebourg* decorative pieces showing the livery of the equipage, as facings it had bands of green caddis on the front of the lining.

The supple boots were made from blackened calf skin with "English-style" kneepads with no incisures and that rolled down over the calves. The adjustable spurs were attached using clamps and underfoot straps. Up to the middle of the 19th century shoes and boots didn't have a left or a right foot. The black canvas gaiters with leather buttons were only worn over the buckled shoes during foot service.

To preserve their outfits, each Dragoon wore a green woollen surtout coat with a small collar. It had ten large buttons in the middle and a small button on the left shoulder strap, as well as one or two buttons on the sleeves. All military grading was shown on the surtout coat. A stable waistcoat with sleeves and without tails made from an old surtout coat, decorated with a dozen small uniform buttons completed the working outfit, as well as the side cap made from an old cloth. The bonnet's turn backs were edged with the distinctive colours with the tip decorated with a crest in green and the same contrasting colour. The tricorn hat was lighter than the helmet was worn during the day, although this is not mentioned in the texts.

The shirt was made from white linen it had "matelote" sleeves on which imitation cuffs were buttoned. The collar fastened at the neck, it was black for all of the regiments. For the mounted troops the gloves were made from sheepskin.

The buffalo hide *ceinturon* belt had white stitching and it was used to carry both the sabre and the bayonet (picture 29). The *giberne* and the haversack remained the same as in the ordinances dated 1753-1754.

Weapons

Most of the regiments maintained the 1750 model sabre. Rifles from 1733 and 1754 were still in use when the ordinance of 1762 appeared. It was only envisaged to renew this dated weapon with the arrival of the 1763-1766 model, that was

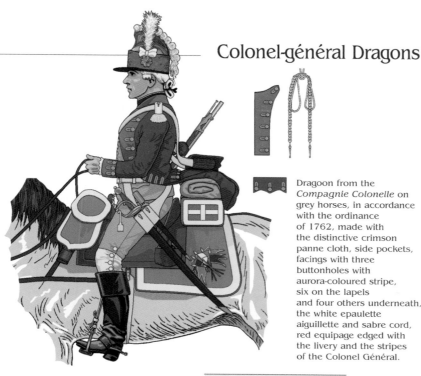

Dragoon from the *Compagnie Colonelle* on grey horses, in accordance with the ordinance of 1762, made with the distinctive crimson panne cloth, side pockets, facings with three buttonholes with aurora-coloured stripe, six on the lapels and four others underneath, the white epaulette aiguillette and sabre cord, red equipage edged with the livery and the stripes of the Colonel Général.

Dragoon wearing fawn jacket decorated with imitation pockets and a shoulder strap in the distinctive colours, in accordance with the ordinance of 1762.

White stripe in chain stich with the 1762 livery.

Yellow button stamped N° 1.

Black stripe edged with red and aurora chains of the 1767 livery.

Captain from the Colonel Général regiment in accordance with the ordinance of 1767.

Dragoon in accordance with the ordinance of 1767 without aiguillette or epaulette, red equipage with a black stripe and red and aurora chains.

produced in 5 000 examples. It was an improvement from the former model with a guidon on the *embouchoir*, a side pin, specific to the Dragoons, the grenadier was made from iron, a red strap and the same bayonet. The arm measured only 153 cm, with a calibre of 17.5 mm, and weighed 3,860 kg.

The 1733 model pistol that was still in use was gradually replaced by the 1763 cavalry model pistol, which was 48 cm long and weighed 1,400 kg. It was followed by the 1763-1766 model that was shorter just 40,2 cm and weighed 1,230 kg.

Equipage and horse tack

In 1764 a new model gradually came into use following replacements and repairs. The saddlecloth and the chaperon were made from Lodève or Berry serge, green or red edged with the regiment's livery and lined with linen. The saddle and the iron pistol on the left and the tool holster on the right were made from natural leather.

At this period the equipage included a rectangular portmanteau the same colour as the saddlecloth and with a canvas bag *(page 48)*.

Bas-officiers (sub-officers or NCOs)

The sub officers wore the same uniform and weapons as the troop except for the *Maréchaux-des-logis* and the Furirs who had a pair of pistols.

The Furir wore a double silver or gold 27 mm stripe across each arm.

The *Maréchal-des-logis* wore a single silver or gold 27 mm wide stripe on the facings.

The *brigadier* wore a double white or yellow woollen stripe, one measuring 40 mm and the other 22 mm.

The *appointé* (**Appointee**) (highly paid former soldier) wore a white or yellow 22 mm stripe on the facings.

The drummers wore a blue outfit with the small King's livery for the royal regiments and with the colonel's livery for regiments belonging to *gentilhommes*. The collar and the facings were of distinctive colours, the lapels, pockets and turn backs were edged with the musicians' livery. Above and below the lapels there were two *Brandebourg* decorative pieces, the pockets had three double buttonholes, the facings and tails had two buttonholes on each side.

Officers

The officers' uniform was the same as the rest of the troop made from serge finer than Elbeuf with the distinctive velvet, silver or gold buttons and buttonholes. Officers from headquarters were recognizable with their gold buttonholes on their jackets and the

white egret on the helmet. Officers also wore a fitted coat when off duty. They were armed with an officer's 1752 model rifle, 145 cm long, a pair of pistols and a smaller giberne decorated with a medallion on the flap. The belt held the "musket-style" sword off duty, or the troop's sabre with a gold mount while on duty. The equipage had two holders, a saddlecloth and two chaperons in serge with a sliver 23 mm stripe or the livery's stripe.

The order of 1762 established ranked epaulettes for all of the officers, with the aiguillette and lanyard in silver or in gold depending on the colour of the buttons.

The colonel wore a bullion fringed epaulette and bowed cords on the left as well as a silver aiguillette on the right.

The lieutenant colonel wore the same epaulette on the left without an aiguillette or an epaulette on the right.

The major wore two silver or gold epaulettes with a simple fringe.

The captain wore an epaulette with a simple fringe in silver or gold on the left hand side.

The lieutenant wore an epaulette with white and silver diamond shapes on the right, and an aiguillette one third in white silk and the other two thirds in silver.

The *Cornette* (sub lieutenant) wore the *aiguillette* on the right, two thirds in white silk and one third in silver, and on the left an epaulette made from squares of white silk and silver fringes. The guidon bearer and the quartermaster wore an aiguillette with two thirds white silk and one third in silver, and an epaulette made from white silk with silver edges.

ORDINANCE FROM APRIL 25th 1767

The ordinance of 1762 was too reformist and could not be put into practise without preliminary tests, that were considerably slowed down by bad habits, and that were often deflected from their original purpose by dishonest suppliers.

A new ordinance was necessary to implement the Duke of Choiseul's reforms on April 25th 1767. This new ordinance was based on the former but contained more detail and was tightly controlled by inspectors.

Outfit

The outfit, little different was tighter, only the aiguillettes and the epaulettes were discarded and replaced by a simple green shoulder strap on the left. The decorative buttonholes below the lapels no longer fastened the outfit over the stomach. The shape of the pocket cuffs remained the same for the regiment of Orléans who wore a coat of arms decorated with 9 buttons. The disposition and distinctive colours were altered as follows:

(Continued on page 38)

Mestre-de-Camp général

Dragoon wearing coat made from whitish-grey serge, with green facing and three *Brandebourgs* with the livery's braid, in accordance with the ordinance of 1762.

Dragoon in accordance with the ordinance of 1762 with the distinctive red colour, side pockets and facings decorated with three aurora-coloured buttonholes, six on the lapels and four underneath, scarlet jacket turn backs, decorative pieces in the colours of the livery, green equipage with braid and stripes of the Mestre-de-Camp Général.

White stripe edged with the livery's aurora-coloured *fleur de lis* in 1762.

Yellow buttons stamped N°2.

Black braid with yellow stripe and red *tablettes*, embroidered with black and yellow chain stiches, with the livery of 1767.

Dragoon in working clothes in accordance with the ordinance of 1767 with the green surtout, the jacket was made from a former surtout and the *"Dragoon–style"* bonnet was decorated with a *fleur de lis* and braid with the distinctive colour.

Dragoon in accordance with the ordinance of 1767, in the distinctive scarlet colour, without any aiguillettes or epaulettes, red equipage edged with the new braid.

27

Royal Dragons, 1762-1767

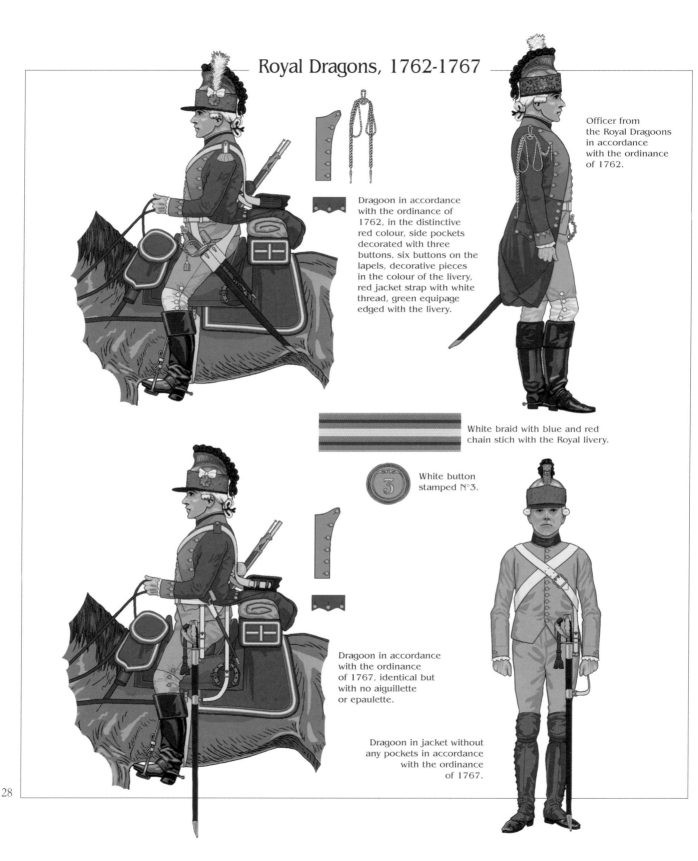

Dragoon in accordance with the ordinance of 1762, in the distinctive red colour, side pockets decorated with three buttons, six buttons on the lapels, decorative pieces in the colour of the livery, red jacket strap with white thread, green equipage edged with the livery.

Officer from the Royal Dragoons in accordance with the ordinance of 1762.

White braid with blue and red chain stich with the Royal livery.

White button stamped N°3.

Dragoon in accordance with the ordinance of 1767, identical but with no aiguillette or epaulette.

Dragoon in jacket without any pockets in accordance with the ordinance of 1767.

Du Roy Dragons

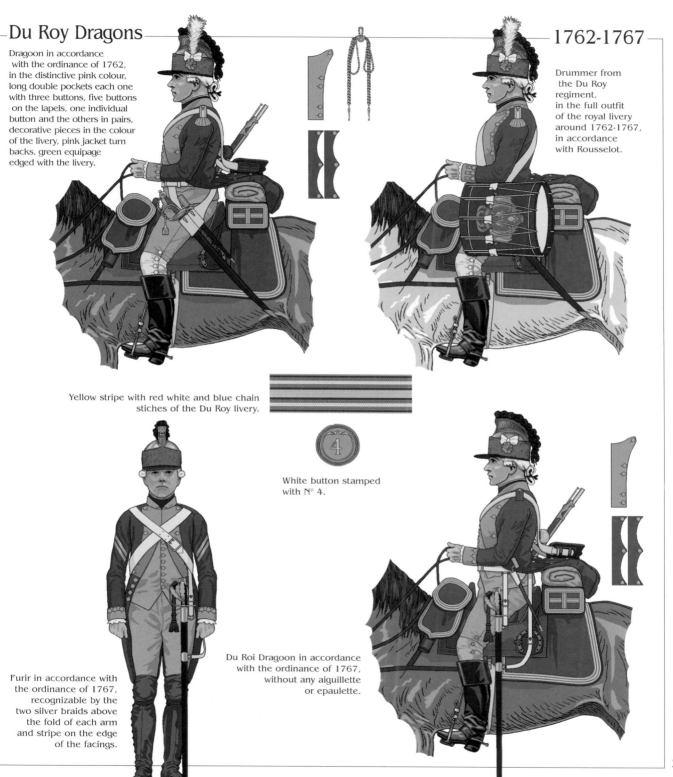

Dragoon in accordance
with the ordinance of 1762,
in the distinctive pink colour,
long double pockets each one
with three buttons, five buttons
on the lapels, one individual
button and the others in pairs,
decorative pieces in the colour
of the livery, pink jacket turn
backs, green equipage
edged with the livery.

Drummer from
the Du Roy
regiment,
in the full outfit
of the royal livery
around 1762-1767,
in accordance
with Rousselot.

Yellow stripe with red white and blue chain
stiches of the Du Roy livery.

White button stamped
with N° 4.

Furir in accordance with
the ordinance of 1767,
recognizable by the
two silver braids above
the fold of each arm
and stripe on the edge
of the facings.

Du Roi Dragoon in accordance
with the ordinance of 1767,
without any aiguillette
or epaulette.

29

La Reine Dragons

Dragoon in infantry
outfit in accordance
with the ordinance
of 1762.

Dragoon in accordance
with the ordinance
of 1762 in the
distinctive violet colour
side pockets decorated
with three buttons,
six buttons on the
lapels, decorative
pieces mixed with
white and blue, pink
jacket turn backs, red
equipage with
the livery braid.

La Reine blue stripe.

White button
stamped N° 5.

Dragoon in surtout and
bonnet, in accordance
with the ordinance
of 1767.

Dragoon in accordance with the
ordinance of 1767 with three small
buttons on the side of the facings
in the distinctive crimson colour.

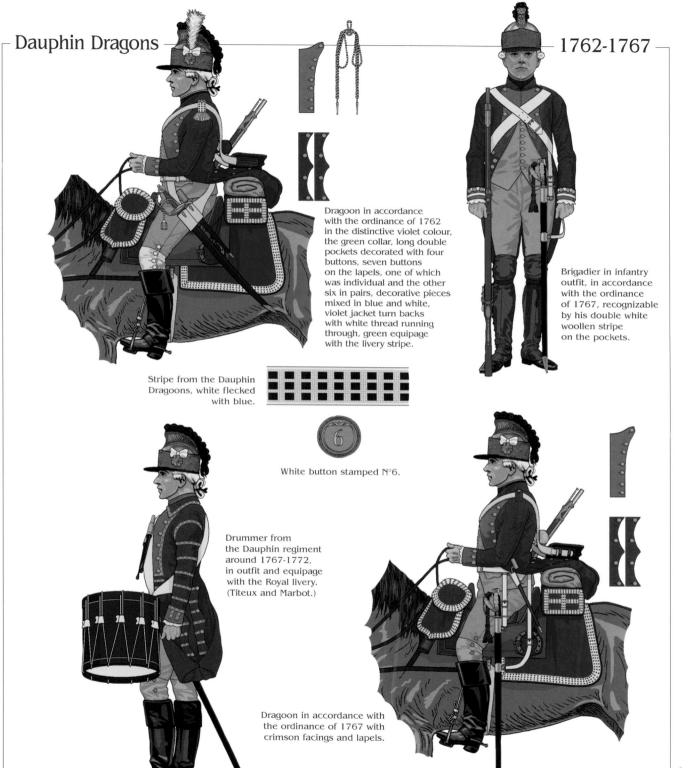

Dragoon in accordance with the ordinance of 1762 in the distinctive violet colour, the green collar, long double pockets decorated with four buttons, seven buttons on the lapels, one of which was individual and the other six in pairs, decorative pieces mixed in blue and white, violet jacket turn backs with white thread running through, green equipage with the livery stripe.

Brigadier in infantry outfit, in accordance with the ordinance of 1767, recognizable by his double white woollen stripe on the pockets.

Stripe from the Dauphin Dragoons, white flecked with blue.

White button stamped N°6.

Drummer from the Dauphin regiment around 1767-1772, in outfit and equipage with the Royal livery. (Titeux and Marbot.)

Dragoon in accordance with the ordinance of 1767 with crimson facings and lapels.

31

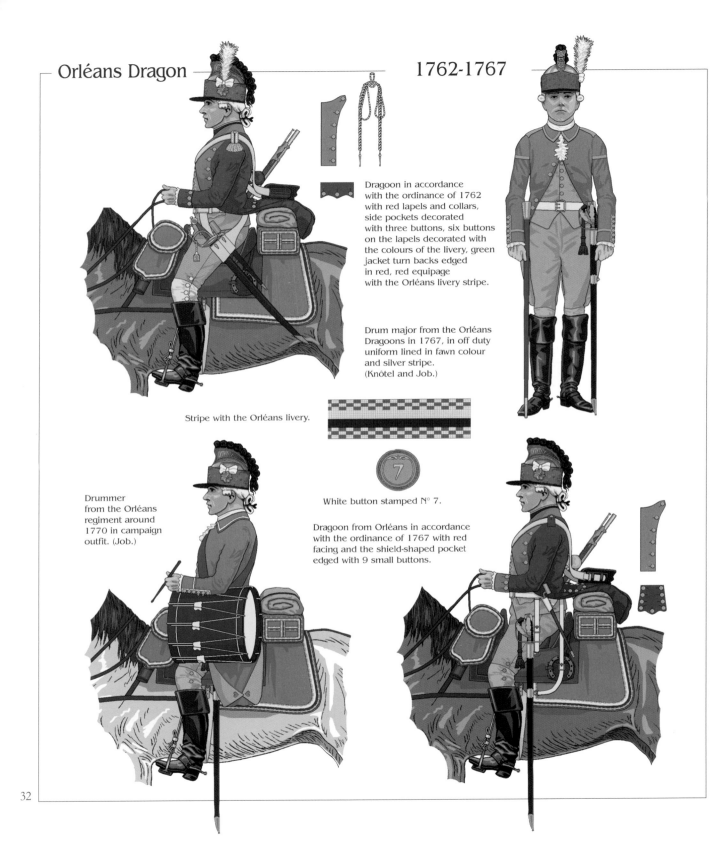

Orléans Dragon

Dragoon in accordance
with the ordinance of 1762
with red lapels and collars,
side pockets decorated
with three buttons, six buttons
on the lapels decorated with
the colours of the livery, green
jacket turn backs edged
in red, red equipage
with the Orléans livery stripe.

Drum major from the Orléans
Dragoons in 1767, in off duty
uniform lined in fawn colour
and silver stripe.
(Knötel and Job.)

Stripe with the Orléans livery.

White button stamped N° 7.

Drummer
from the Orléans
regiment around
1770 in campaign
outfit. (Job.)

Dragoon from Orléans in accordance
with the ordinance of 1767 with red
facing and the shield-shaped pocket
edged with 9 small buttons.

Beaufremont Dragons

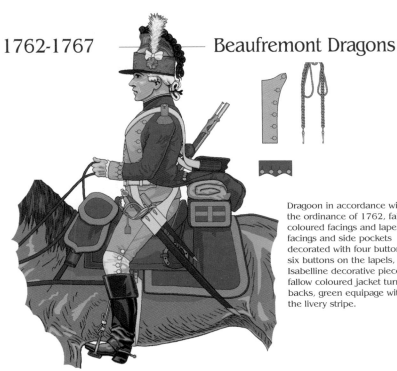

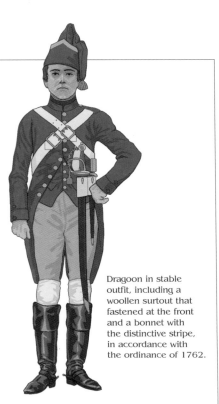

Dragoon in accordance with the ordinance of 1762, fallow coloured facings and lapels, facings and side pockets decorated with four buttons, six buttons on the lapels, Isabelline decorative pieces, fallow coloured jacket turn backs, green equipage with the livery stripe.

Dragoon in stable outfit, including a woollen surtout that fastened at the front and a bonnet with the distinctive stripe, in accordance with the ordinance of 1762.

Isabelline stripe with the Beauffremont livery.

White button stamped N° 8.

Dragoon in coat with hood to protect the helmet and the distinctive Isabelline *Brandebourgs*, in accordance with the ordinance of 1767.

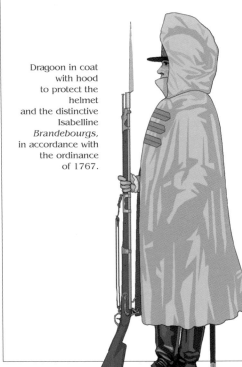

Dragoon in accordance with the ordinance of 1767, identical but without any aiguillettes or epaulettes.

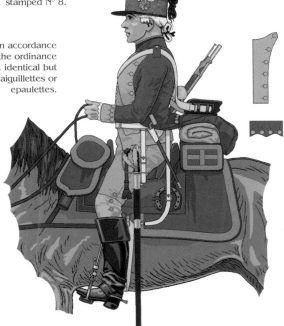

Choiseul & Custine Dragons, 1762-1767

Dragoon from the Choiseul and Custine Dragoons
in accordance with the ordinance of 1762, in the
distinctive yellow lemon colour, long double pockets
and facings decorated with four buttons,
six on the lapels, decorative
pieces in the livery's
colours, yellow
lemon jacket turn
backs, green
equipage with
the livery's stripe.

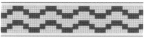

White stripe with crimson *zig zag*
decorative pieces (*lézardes*)
of the regiment's livery.

The guidons from the Custine Dragoons from 1763-1780
were embroidered and fringed in gold, on the blue obverse,
the sun and the royal motto, on the crimson reverse
the allegory of a silver centaur and the motto
IN UTROQUE TREMENDUS
(Pajol and Montigny).

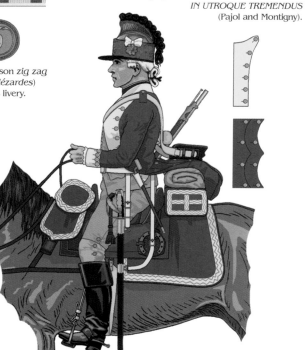

Custine Dragoon
in accordance with
the ordinance of 1767,
wearing identical uniform
without any aiguillettes
or epaulettes.

Dragoon in outfit for
marching in accordance
with the ordinance of 1767.

34

Autichamps Dragons, 1762-67

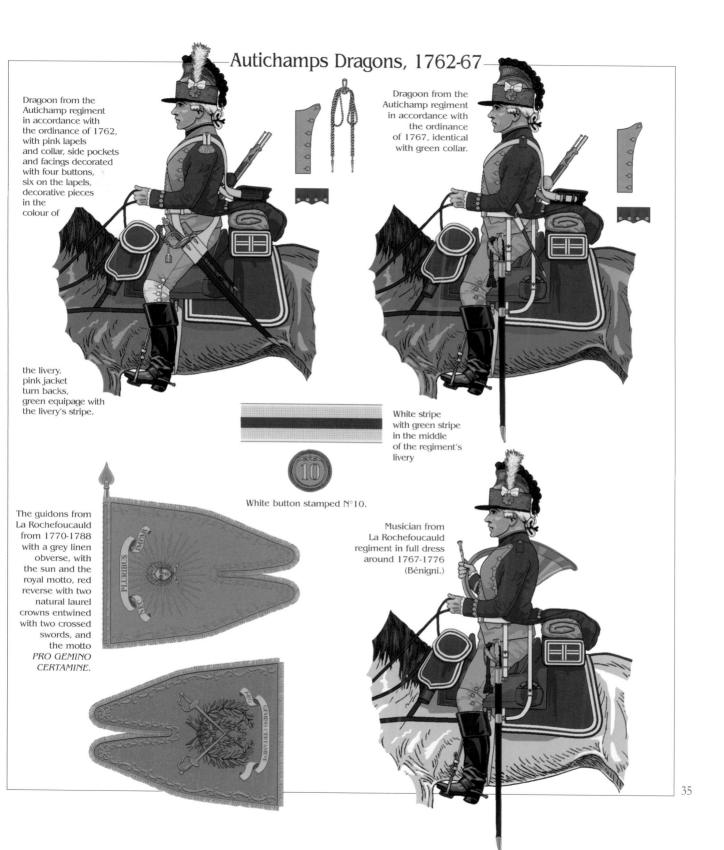

Dragoon from the Autichamp regiment in accordance with the ordinance of 1762, with pink lapels and collar, side pockets and facings decorated with four buttons, six on the lapels, decorative pieces in the colour of

the livery, pink jacket turn backs, green equipage with the livery's stripe.

Dragoon from the Autichamp regiment in accordance with the ordinance of 1767, identical with green collar.

White stripe with green stripe in the middle of the regiment's livery

White button stamped N°10.

The guidons from La Rochefoucauld from 1770-1788 with a grey linen obverse, with the sun and the royal motto, red reverse with two natural laurel crowns entwined with two crossed swords, and the motto *PRO GEMINO CERTAMINE.*

Musician from La Rochefoucauld regiment in full dress around 1767-1776 (Bénigni.)

PLURIBUS IMPAR

NEC

PRO GEMINO CERTAMINE

1762-1767

Dragoon in accordance with the ordinance of 1762, in the distinctive fallow-colour, long double pockets and facings decorated with three buttons, seven on the lapels, six of them

Chabot and Jarnac regiments from 1762_1782 had the same guidons, embroidered and fringed in gold and silver, with on the red obverse the sun and the royal motto, and on the white reverse with the Arms of the House of Chabot (gold Coat of Arms with three Chabot fish as gules) and the motto *IN UTROQUE TREMENDOUS* (Lemau and Pajol).

in pairs, decorative pieces in the livery's colours, fallow-coloured jacket turn backs, green equipage with the livery's stripe.

White button stamped N° 11.

White braid with double crimson stripe with the regiment's livery.

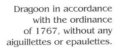

Dragoon in accordance with the ordinance of 1767, without any aiguillettes or epaulettes.

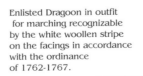

Enlisted Dragoon in outfit for marching recognizable by the white woollen stripe on the facings in accordance with the ordinance of 1762-1767.

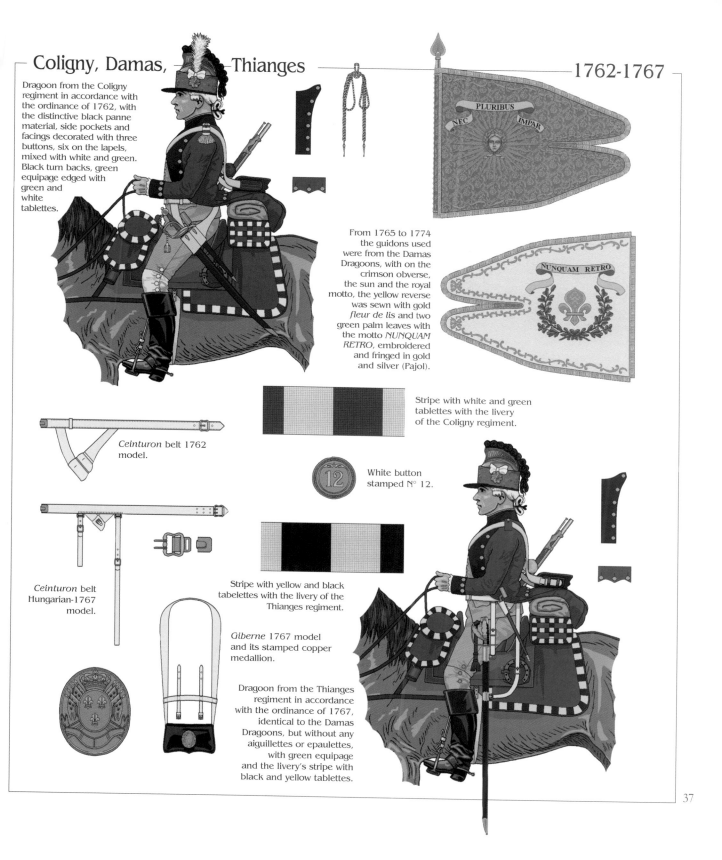

Dragoon from the Coligny regiment in accordance with the ordinance of 1762, with the distinctive black panne material, side pockets and facings decorated with three buttons, six on the lapels, mixed with white and green. Black turn backs, green equipage edged with green and white tablettes.

PLURIBUS NEC IMPAR

From 1765 to 1774 the guidons used were from the Damas Dragoons, with on the crimson obverse, the sun and the royal motto, the yellow reverse was sewn with gold *fleur de lis* and two green palm leaves with the motto *NUNQUAM RETRO*, embroidered and fringed in gold and silver (Pajol).

NUNQUAM RETRO

Stripe with white and green tablettes with the livery of the Coligny regiment.

Ceinturon belt 1762 model.

White button stamped N° 12.

Ceinturon belt Hungarian-1767 model.

Stripe with yellow and black tabelettes with the livery of the Thianges regiment.

Giberne 1767 model and its stamped copper medallion.

Dragoon from the Thianges regiment in accordance with the ordinance of 1767, identical to the Damas Dragoons, but without any aiguillettes or epaulettes, with green equipage and the livery's stripe with black and yellow tablettes.

— *Colonel-General*, crimson lapels, facings and collar, *Mestre-de-Camp*, red lapels, facings and collar, *Royal*, red lapels, facings and collar, *Du Roy*, dark pink lapels, facings and collar, *La Reine*, crimson lapels, facings and collar, *Dauphin*, crimson lapels, facings and green collar, *Orléans*, red lapels, facings and red collar, *Beauffremont*, buck-coloured lapels and facings, green collar, *Custine*, lemon yellow lapels and facings, *La Rochefoucauld*, pink lapels, green facings and collar, *Chabot*, buck-coloured lapels, facings and collar, *Thianges*, black lapels, facings and collar, *Lanan*, aurora lapels, facings and collar, *Belsunce*, scarlet lapels and facings, green collar, *Monteclerc*, aurora lapels and facings, green collar, *Languedoc*, fawn lapels and collar, green facings, *Schomberg*, scarlet lapels, facings and collar.

The jacket was altered, pockets and shoulder straps were removed, and the *"Bavarian–style"* leather culottes with side pockets on the waistband, and cuffs and stockings were knitted in a grey slate colour. There was no official model for helmets, the specific model of each regiment remained until the end of the regime. The horses were powdered on Sundays and for parades, tails knotted and raised with the sides rolled. Boots, gaiters and in particular the waistcoat complied with the ordinance of 1762, as well as the bonnet that was decorated with a fleur-de-lis sewn on the front.

The coat had three *brandebourg* decorative pieces in serge in the regiment's distinctive colours. The black collar could be red only if the coat's collar was not the same colour. The equipages and tack conformed with the 1764 regulations.

A new blackened giberne made from cowhide contained a pierced square box with 30 cartridges. The seamless flap was decorated with a large brass medallion stamped with the King's arms. Under the flap was the leather bag to store flint and other oily parts. The giberne's strap was made from whitened buffalo hide and it buckled at the side of the box. There was a buffalo hide crosspiece sewn onto the strap to carry the coat's hood.

The "Hungarian-style" *ceinturon* belt was chosen to keep the 1767 model sabre taken from the *volontaires* corps. It was made from boiled buffalo hide, it had two holders for sabres, a brass shield with an *ardillon* and an iron chape open to attach the hook sewn onto the other side of the belt. A bayonet *"hunting knife"* pendant was sewn into the belt between the two leather rings *(page 37)*. On foot service the belt was worn around the neck.

Weapons

In 1764, the sabre with a *"demi-basket shaped"* mount and thumb stall from Aubigné became the main model for future productions. This kind of sabre was made in various forms including the 1766-67 model with a full basket shaped mount with five iron branches, a straight flat back blade. The most common model was the one mentioned in the 1767 ordinance, with a mount in demi-basket shape with two branches in flat iron, without a thumb guard, a flat straight blade measuring 97.5 cm, a scabbard in blackened leather with a chape and an iron ring and a brass tip. The sabre's cord that would become the future lanyard was in blackened leather with a small crest.

The 1763-1766 model rifle proposed as a second manufacture, was designated as the 1766/70 model, it was produced with a 1770 type lock, a butt but no *busc*, there was a short *embouchoir* and a tenon below the canon to put the ferrule bayonet model 1770.

The pistol was the same as the cavalry model from 1763.

Bas-officiers (sub-officers or NCOs)

The Furir wore two 27 mm silver or gold stripes across each arm and the same striped edge on the facings. In charge of the camp, he carried a long 2 m pole with the regiment's distinctive colours.

The *Maréchal-des-logis* wore a single silver or gold stripe on the facings.

The *brigadier* wore a double white or yellow stripe depending on the colour of the buttons on the facings, from one another 40 mm to 22 mm.

The *appointé* wore 22 mm white or yellow stripe on the facings.

The re-enlisted soldier wore one or two 22 mm white or gold stripes. From 1771, a third engagement after 24 years of service was shown by a brass and red serge medallion for veterans, worn on the right hand side of the chest.

The drummers'outfits conformed with the ordinance of 1762.

Officers

The new ordinance stipulated no changes to the officers'outfits, the 1767 model sabre for the cavalry officers and Dragoons however became the first regulatory arm, the mount had three branches in polished iron, a back blade measuring 92 to 97.5 cm, and a leather scabbard with iron decorations.

The colonel wore two epaulettes with bullion fringes and cord bows on the left.

The lieutenant colonel, the major, the captain and the lieutenant wore the same rank distinctions as in 1762, but with no aiguillettes.

The Cornet (or second Lieutenant) wore a silk epaulette with the distinctive colours, with squares and silver fringes on the left.

Dragoon from the Nicolaï regiment in accordance with the ordinance of 1762, in the distinctive aurora-colour, facings and side pockets decorated with four buttons, six buttons on the reverse, blue and aurora coloured decorative pieces, aurora jacket turn backs, green equipage with the regiment's stripe.

The Nicolaï Dragoons were definitely those from the Apchon Dragoons with green backing *(page 20)*.

Arms of the Marquis of Nicolaï, crowned silver greyhound on the azure Coat of Arms.

Guidons from the Lanan Dragoons from 1763 to 1782 made from grey linen, the obverse illustrated the sun and the royal motto, and a crimson reverse, undoubtedly with the Count's Arms, gules with band of gold fleur-de-lis (*Dictionnaire de la Noblesse de France* 1821 and Marbot).

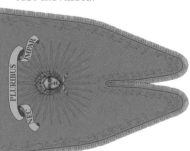

The regiment's blue and aurora-coloured tablette stripe.

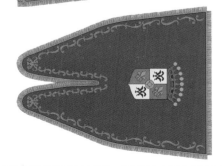

White button decorated N° 13.

Dragoon from the Lanan regiment in accordance with the ordinance of 1767, identical to the Nicolaï regiment.

The guidon bearer and the quarter master wore a silk epaulette with the distinctive colours and silver edging on the left.

ORDINANCE FROM MAY 31ST 1776

On April 17th 1772, all of the 17 regiments were organised into 12 companies of 32 Dragoons and mounted sub officers, 8 infantry, making a total number of 384 men, 228 of whom were mounted and 96 of whom were infantry, and for the entire arm there were 6 528 men. Named as the War Minister in 1775, the Count of Saint-Germain undertook numerous reforms, including 98 ordinances in just two years, with the aim of modernising Louis XVI's army. Measures included the reduction of the *Maison de sa Majesté*, doubling the number of infantry and cavalry and including the *Milice* and provincial regiments, the abolishment of the venality of responsibilities, the creation of twelve military schools open to abecedarians, accessible to superior ranks from disinherited aristocracy, the return of religion into teaching, these numerous measures gave the army a new boost.

The Royal ordinance from March 25th 1776 concerned the Dragoons in particular, officially assimilating them with the cavalry, transferring into its ranks the cavalry regiments of Chartres, Condé, Bourbon, Conti, La Marche, Penthièvre and Noailles. The ranking order of the Dragoon's 24 regiments was modified, respecting the date of entry into the ranking. The Royal regiments were in first position, Colonel-Général, Mestre-de-Camp-Général, Royal, Du Roy, La Reine, Dauphin, followed by the regiments *Princes du sang* and *gentilshommes*, Monsieur, Artois, Orléans, Chartres, Condé, Bourbon, Conti, Penthièvre, Boufflers, Lorraine, Custine, La Rochefoucauld, Jarnac, Lanan, Belsunce, Languedoc, Noailles, and Schomberg.

Each regiment made up of four squadrons to a company was provided with a fifth squadron. Similar to the light horses in the cavalry, the 5th Dragoon squadron was comprised of two companies of mounted chasseurs, from Flanders, Morraine, Condé, Soubise and the Dauphiné regions. A sixth auxiliary squadron was formed in time of war, and included men aged between 18 and 25, and who measured over 1m70.

All of the squadrons were made up of 60 Dragoons and mounted sub officers and 40 infantry soldiers, totally 500 men, 300 of whom were on horseback and 200 on foot for each regiment, totally 12 000 men for the arm. The first two squadrons in each regiment were under the command of a *Mestre-de-Camp* in second and a Lieutenant – Colonel in second. Each squadron had 1 commanding captain, 1 captain in second, 1 first lieutenant, 1 second lieutenant, 2 sub-lieutenants; 1 *Maréchal-des-logis* in chief, 1 second *Maréchal-des-logis*, 1 Furir-writer, 8 brigadiers, 1 *cadet-gentilhomme* (aged from 15 to 20), 152

Dragoons or chasseurs, 2 trumpeters 1 frater (assistant surgeon), 1 farrier, in total 174 men, including officers.

The regiment's headquarters included 1 commanding *Mestre-de-camp* (chief of the corps), 1 *Mestre-de-camp* in second (second in chief of corps), 1 lieutenant-colonel (in charge of administration), 1 major (captain in charge of manoeuvers, discipline and uniform), 1 treasurer quarter master (lieutenant), 2 guidon-bearers (*Maréchaux-des-logis* or furirs), 1 adjutant (first *Maréchal-des-logis* in chief), 1 surgeon-major (officially part of the corps since 1772), 1 chaplain, 1 master farrier (*Maréchal-des-logis*), 1 master saddler (*Maréchal-des-logis*) & 1 armourer (since 1775).

The posts of assistant-major and sub -major, quartermaster, one of the three guidon–bearers, furirs and appointées were abolished, as well as the posts of Captain–lieutenant, sub-lieutenants and cornets for companies from the *Colonel-Général* and *Mestre-de-Camp* regiments.

The Dragoons continued to wear uniforms that had been previously regulated, as did the cavalry regiments who remained part of the Dragoon corps awaiting new ordinances. The chasseurs forming the 5th squadron, wore the same uniform as the Dragoons with a saddlecloth showing the Royal livery.

On December 25th 1778, all of the 5 squadrons had 70 Dragoons and mounted sub officers, and 30 infantry, with the same total.

The talented drummers from the mounted companies became trumpeters or simple Dragoons. The Drum majors became *Maréchal-des-logis*. All of the posts of timpanists from the old regiments were abolished.

Uniforms

In accordance with the ordinance of May 31st 1776, and as a result of the double numbers in the infantry regiments, it was decided to allocate a second distinctive regimental colour on the outfits, one on the collar, and the other on the facings, lapels and lining, as the following:

— *Colonel-Général*, distinctive colour and collar scarlet, *Mestre-de-camp*, green collar and scarlet distinctive colour, *Royal*, distinctive colour scarlet and white collar, *Du Roi*, distinctive colour and collar dark pink, *La Reine*, distinctive colour crimson and white collar, *Dauphin*, distinctive colour crimson and yellow collar, *Monsieur*, distinctive colour scarlet, yellow collar, *Artois*, distinctive colour pink and white collar, *Orléans*, distinctive colour pink, and white collar, *Chartres*, distinctive colour red, and white collar, *Condé*, distinctive colour and collar chamois-Condé, *Bourbon*, red collar and distinctive colour chamois-Condé, *Conti*, distinctive colour chamois-Conti and pink collar, *Penthièvre*,

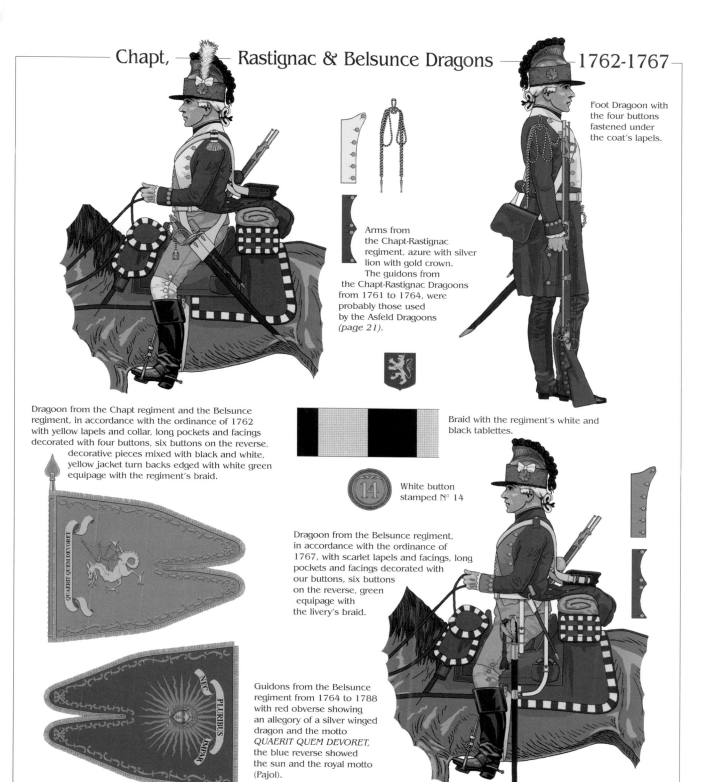

Foot Dragoon with the four buttons fastened under the coat's lapels.

Arms from the Chapt-Rastignac regiment, azure with silver lion with gold crown. The guidons from the Chapt-Rastignac Dragoons from 1761 to 1764, were probably those used by the Asfeld Dragoons (page 21).

Dragoon from the Chapt regiment and the Belsunce regiment, in accordance with the ordinance of 1762 with yellow lapels and collar, long pockets and facings decorated with four buttons, six buttons on the reverse, decorative pieces mixed with black and white, yellow jacket turn backs edged with white green equipage with the regiment's braid.

Braid with the regiment's white and black tablettes.

White button stamped N° 14

Dragoon from the Belsunce regiment, in accordance with the ordinance of 1767, with scarlet lapels and facings, long pockets and facings decorated with our buttons, six buttons on the reverse, green equipage with the livery's braid.

QUAERIT QUEM DEVORET

NEC PLURIBUS IMPAR

Guidons from the Belsunce regiment from 1764 to 1788 with red obverse showing an allegory of a silver winged dragon and the motto QUAERIT QUEM DEVORET, the blue reverse showed the sun and the royal motto (Pajol).

distinctive colour and collar yellow, *Boufflers*, distinctive colour chamois-Conti and pink collar, *Lorraine*, distinctive colour red and yellow collar, *Custine*, distinctive colour yellow and collar scarlet, *La Rochefoucauld*, distinctive colour pink and collar yellow, *Jarnac*, distinctive colour and collar white, *Lanan*, distinctive colour and collar aurora, *Belsunce*, distinctive colour white and collar scarlet, *Languedoc*, distinctive colour aurora and green collar, *Noailles*, distinctive colour white and pink collar, *Schomberg*, distinctive colour aurora and yellow collar.

The lapels were decorated with 7 small equally-spaced buttons, with four buttons and buttonholes below. The open facings were decorated with four buttonholes, two on the facing and two on the forearm sleeve. The open turn backs covered the pockets that were either cut to the side or lengthwise, and bordered and lined in the distinctive regimental colour.

The tails were lined with serge or caddis in the distinctive regimental colour, they were attached and decorated with *fleurs de lis* cut from green serge.

The shoulders were decorated with a green strap that fastened with a button near to the collar which was sewn into the sleeve seam.

The buttons were made from yellow or white metal, banded and stamped with the regiment's number or the Coat of Arms of *Princes du sang*.

The collar of the black ribbed crepe was lined with an apparent white material. The sleeve cuffs were only authorised for the sub officers.

Boots, gaiters, coat, jacket, animal-hide culottes, bonnet, *ceinturon* belt, *giberne* and portmanteau maintained the same forms and size as those previously mentioned. However sub officers and Dragoons wore jackets and culottes made from white material in the summer as long as maintenance was possible.

In addition to the outfits mentioned above, each Dragoon had a long *marnière-style* culottes, and a cream working smock to use in the stables.

The sub officers replaced their used helmets by a hat, that are still in use. Their hair was tied back in a ponytail.

Weapons

The ordinance of 1776, had no effect on the Dragoon weapons already regulated in 1762 and in 1767. The sub officers and Dragoons were armed with just one pistol whereas the Maréchal-des-logis and the Furir had two each.

The Montmorency regiment had a sabre model 1776, unique to this corps'tradition since 1745, they kept it until the Empire. The sabre had a 1767 – style demi-basket mount, with a curved blade *"à la Montmorency"*, measuring 97.5 cm, a scabbard in darkened leather with an iron chape and locket, reinforced with brass lockets and chains.

As from 1778 the new rifle model 1777, which was manufactured up to year XI, was adopted in accordance with the new measures from the new Gribeauval weapon system, it measured 146 cm, brass decoration and an iron grenadier and the strap in leather from Russia.

The pistol *"à coffre"* model 1777 was an original design, and was mass produced, it gradually replaced the model 1763, and the model was finally adopted in year IX.

Equipage and horse tack

The use of saddlecloths was maintained but the chaperons were abolished and replaced by sheep skin shabracks, that were large enough to protect the pistol. The saddle was usually covered with a woollen cover folded to cover the pommel. The bridle, reins, halter and other saddle equipment were the same shape and size as those regulated before ¬1764. From this period, all of the horses were marked with the regiment's number on the left buttock with an iron *(page 48)*.

Bas-officiers (sub-officers or NCOs)

The adjutant wore an epaulette on a flame-coloured silk backing, with two pleated or silver cords running lengthwise, gold, silver or flame-coloured fringes. On the right an identical counter-epaulette was buttoned, without any fringes (picture **56**).

The *Maréchal-des-logis* in chief chef wore on his sleeve, a double gold or silver 22 mm stripe, one on the lower forearm and the other on the facing.

The *Maréchal-des-logis* in second wore a single gold or silver stripe on the forearm above the facing of each sleeve.

The *Furir-writer* wore two gold or silver stripes, sewn sideways above the fold in the arm.

The *brigadier* wore a double stripe in white or yellow wool, above the facings.

The *cadet-gentilhomme* wore two epaulets without fringes in gold or silver braid.

The frater had buttonholes on each facing in yellow or white woollen braid.

The farrier wore on the outside of each sleeve above the arm fold, a horseshoe braided with thread or white or yellow wool.

The reenlisted wore the same chevrons and medallions as in 1767.

The trumpeters wore blue outfits with the livery of the King, collar, lapels, facings and lining in the distinctive colour

(Continued on page 52)

Chabrillan & Monteclerc Dragons, 1762-1767

Arms from the Count of Chabrillan

Dragoon from the Chabrillan regiment and the Monteclerc regiment, in accordance with the ordinance of 1762, with the aurora-coloured lapels and facings, facings and long pockets decorated with three buttons, six buttons on the reverse, sewn individually, in pairs and in threes, decorative pieces in the livery's colours, aurora-coloured jacket turn back edged with white, green equipage edged with livery's braid.

Maréchal-des-logis in dress for marching, recognizable by his silver stripe on the facings in accordance with the ordinance of 1767.

Violet braid with the regiment's livery white edging.

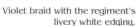

White button stamped N° 15.

Dragoon from the Monteclerc regiment, in accordance with the ordinance of 1767, identical to 1762 model.

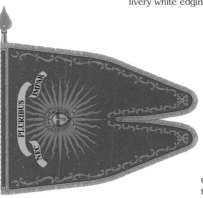

Guidons from the Monteclerc regiment from 1763 to 1774 were probably crimson, embroidered and fringed in gold with the sun and the royal motto on the obverse and the Arms of the Chevalier of Monteclerc on the reverse, with the motto *MAGNUS INTER PARES* (Pajol).

Dragoon in accordance with the ordinance of 1762, with white lapels and collar, facings and long pockets decorated with four buttons, six buttons on the reverse in pairs, four buttons below in pairs, decorated with the livery's colours, white jacket turn backs, green equipage edged with livery's braid.

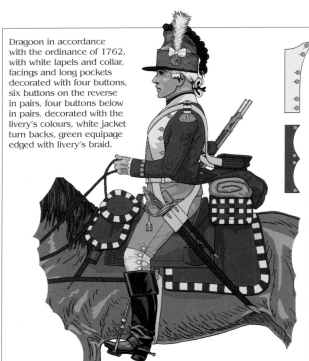

The guidons from the Languedoc regiment from 1770 to 1791 were embroidered and fringed in gold and silver, blue damas on one side showing the golden faced sun, silver rays and the royal motto, the other side was in yellow damas with the Arms of the Provence of Languedoc (from the *Carnets de la Sabretache*).

Blue and white tablettes on the livery's braid.

White button stamped N° 16.

Dragoon in accordance with the ordinance of 1767, with fawn coloured lapels and collar, facings and long pockets decorated with four buttons, six buttons on the reverse in pairs, green equipage edged with the livery's braid.

Dragoon wearing coat with Brandebourg decorative pieces on the hood and the regiment's distinctive colours, in accordance with the ordinance of 1767.

Schomberg Dragons, 1762-1767

Dragoon from the Schomberg regiment wearing coat in 1762 with three of the livery's *Brandebourgs* decorative pieces. (Rousselot.)

Dragoon in accordance with the ordinance of 1762, with the distinctive scarlet colour, green facings and side pocket s decorated with three buttons, seven buttons on the reverse in pairs, decorated with the livery's colours, scarlet jacket turn backs with fallow – coloured edging, green equipage edged with the livery's braid.

The Schomberg guidons from 1762-1791 were fringed and embroidered in gold, on the blue obverse, the sun and the royal motto, on the red reverse the Arms of Schomberg (silver heart-shaped Coat of Arms with gold *fleurdelisé* crossed staffs, on azure backing with cavalier armed with sabre) bearing the motto *MENTE MAGNIFICAT* (Pajol).

Livery's stripe on aurora backing and double black *zig zag* decorative pieces

White button stamped N° 17.

Dragoon from the Schomberg regiment with the regiment's distinctive scarlet colour in accordance with the ordinance of 1767.

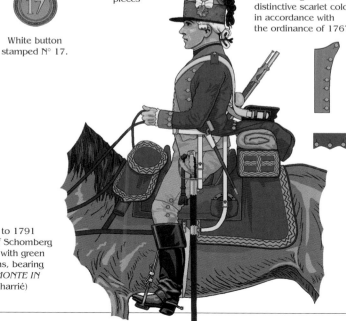

From 1776 to 1791 the Arms of Schomberg were silver, with green and red lions, bearing the motto *MONTE IN PUGNAS* (Charrié)

Colonel-général Dragons — 1776-1786

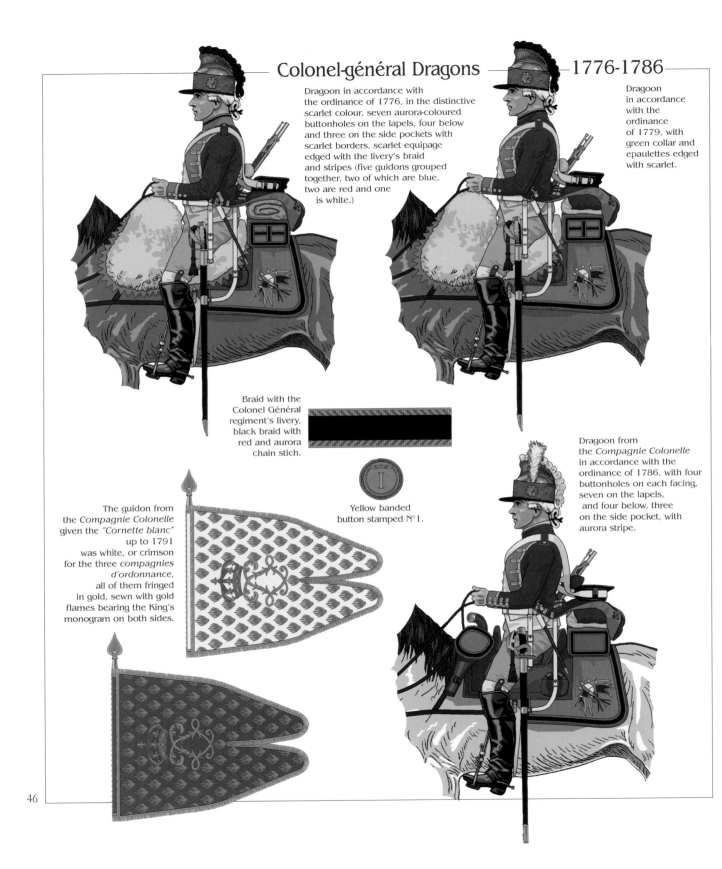

Dragoon in accordance with the ordinance of 1776, in the distinctive scarlet colour, seven aurora-coloured buttonholes on the lapels, four below and three on the side pockets with scarlet borders, scarlet equipage edged with the livery's braid and stripes (five guidons grouped together, two of which are blue, two are red and one is white.)

Dragoon in accordance with the ordinance of 1779, with green collar and epaulettes edged with scarlet.

Braid with the Colonel Général regiment's livery, black braid with red and aurora chain stich.

Yellow banded button stamped N°1.

The guidon from the *Compagnie Colonelle* given the *"Cornette blanc"* up to 1791 was white, or crimson for the three *compagnies d'ordonnance*, all of them fringed in gold, sewn with gold flames bearing the King's monogram on both sides.

Dragoon from the *Compagnie Colonelle* in accordance with the ordinance of 1786, with four buttonholes on each facing, seven on the lapels, and four below, three on the side pocket, with aurora stripe.

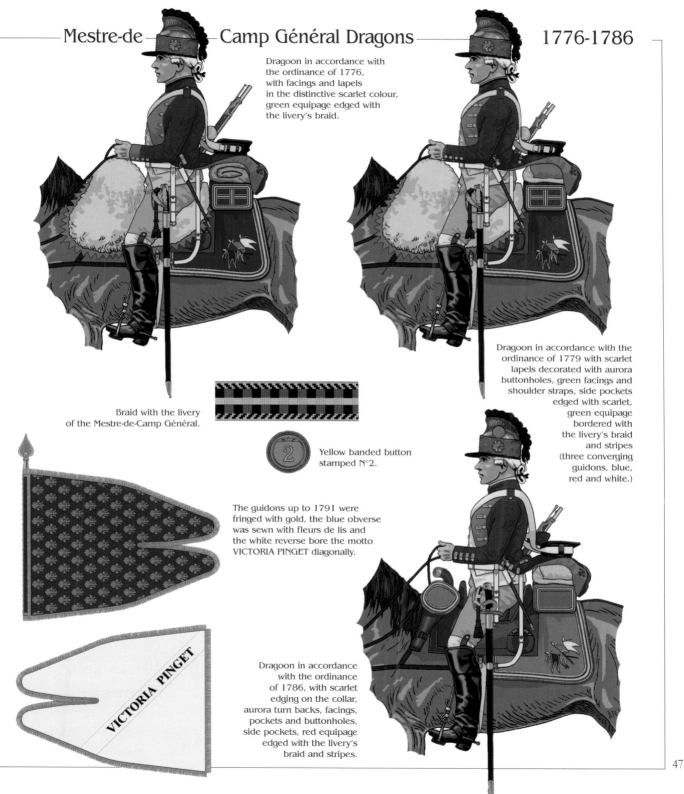

Dragoon in accordance with the ordinance of 1776, with facings and lapels in the distinctive scarlet colour, green equipage edged with the livery's braid.

Braid with the livery of the Mestre-de-Camp Général.

Yellow banded button stamped N°2.

Dragoon in accordance with the ordinance of 1779 with scarlet lapels decorated with aurora buttonholes, green facings and shoulder straps, side pockets edged with scarlet, green equipage bordered with the livery's braid and stripes (three converging guidons, blue, red and white.)

The guidons up to 1791 were fringed with gold, the blue obverse was sewn with fleurs de lis and the white reverse bore the motto VICTORIA PINGET diagonally.

VICTORIA PINGET

Dragoon in accordance with the ordinance of 1786, with scarlet edging on the collar, aurora turn backs, facings, pockets and buttonholes, side pockets, red equipage edged with the livery's braid and stripes.

47

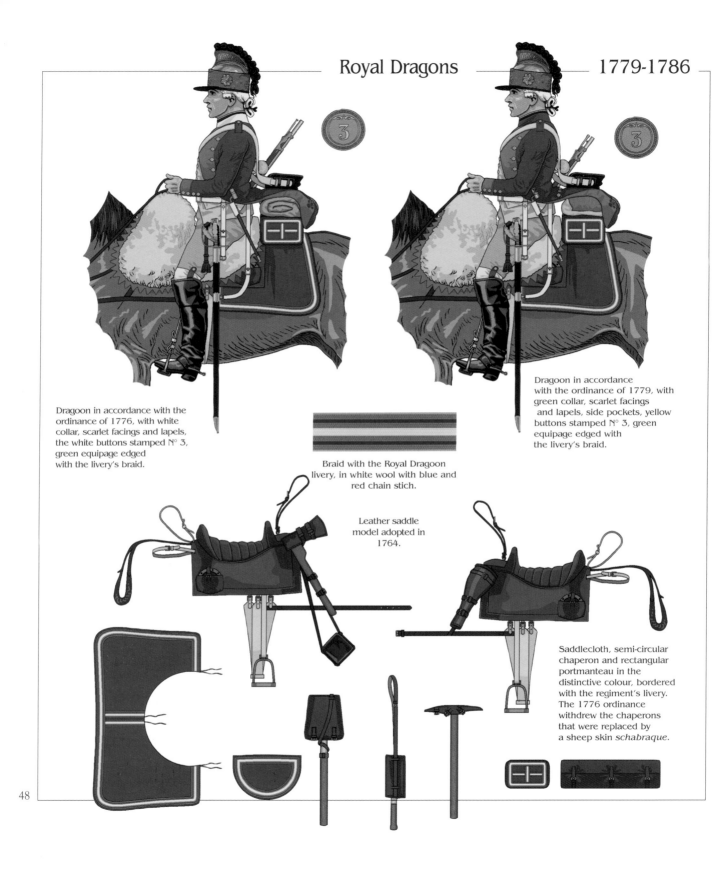

Dragoon in accordance with the ordinance of 1776, with white collar, scarlet facings and lapels, the white buttons stamped N° 3, green equipage edged with the livery's braid.

Dragoon in accordance with the ordinance of 1779, with green collar, scarlet facings and lapels, side pockets, yellow buttons stamped N° 3, green equipage edged with the livery's braid.

Braid with the Royal Dragoon livery, in white wool with blue and red chain stich.

Leather saddle model adopted in 1764.

Saddlecloth, semi-circular chaperon and rectangular portmanteau in the distinctive colour, bordered with the regiment's livery. The 1776 ordinance withdrew the chaperons that were replaced by a sheep skin *schabraque*.

1776-79

"Hungarian" style *Ceinturon* belt and *giberne* in accordance with the ordinance of 1786.

Infantry Dragoon in accordance with the ordinance of 1786.

Dragoon in accordance with the ordinance of 1786 with a white jacket that fastened with eight buttons at the front and a green bonnet bordered in the distinctive colours.

The guidons from the Royal Dragoons had a blue obverse and reverse fringed with gold and silver, with the sun and the royal motto on a blue backing sewn with *fleurs de lis.*

Livery's stripe and yellow button from the Royal Dragoons.

Trumpeter from the Royal Dragons in full dress in accordance with the ordinance of 1786, with the King's livery, blue backing decorated with white cord on red backing.

Dragoon in accordance with the ordinance of 1786 with sc arlet facings and lapels, side pockets, yellow buttons stamped N° 3, green equipage bordered with the livery.

49

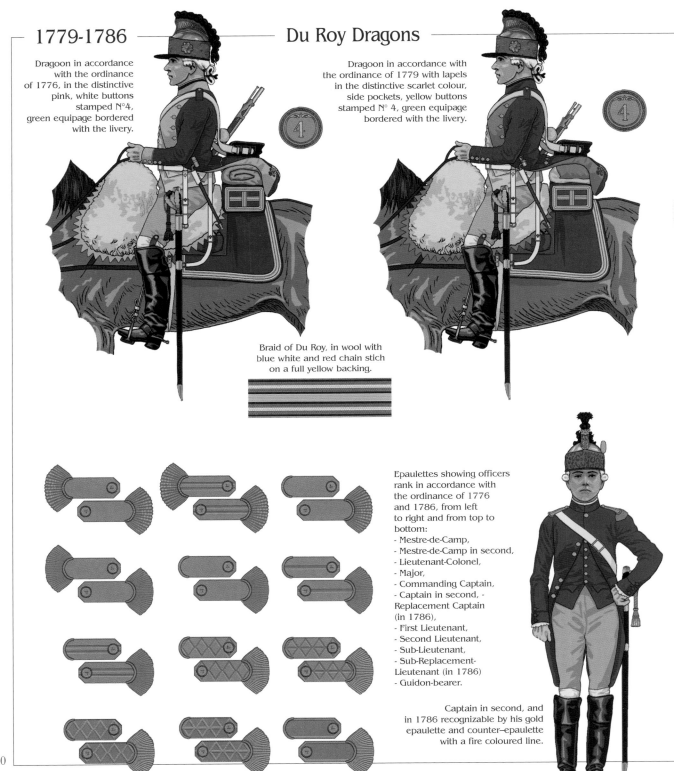

Dragoon in accordance with the ordinance of 1776, in the distinctive pink, white buttons stamped N°4, green equipage bordered with the livery.

Dragoon in accordance with the ordinance of 1779 with lapels in the distinctive scarlet colour, side pockets, yellow buttons stamped N° 4, green equipage bordered with the livery.

Braid of Du Roy, in wool with blue white and red chain stich on a full yellow backing.

Epaulettes showing officers rank in accordance with the ordinance of 1776 and 1786, from left to right and from top to bottom:
- Mestre-de-Camp,
- Mestre-de-Camp in second,
- Lieutenant-Colonel,
- Major,
- Commanding Captain,
- Captain in second, -
Replacement Captain
(in 1786),
- First Lieutenant,
- Second Lieutenant,
- Sub-Lieutenant,
- Sub-Replacement-
Lieutenant (in 1786)
- Guidon-bearer.

Captain in second, and in 1786 recognizable by his gold epaulette and counter–epaulette with a fire coloured line.

Officer in coat made from green serge with collar bordered with braid the same colour as the buttons and the distinctive-coloured facings, in accordance with the ordinance of 1786.

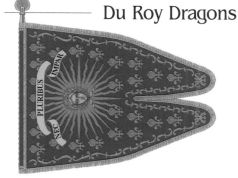

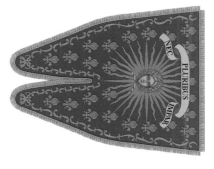

Guidons from the Du Roy regiment 1772-1791, were embroidered and fringed with gold, with both sides in blue sewn with *fleurs de lis*, bearing the sun and the royal motto.

Officer in town outfit in 1786. (Rousselot.)

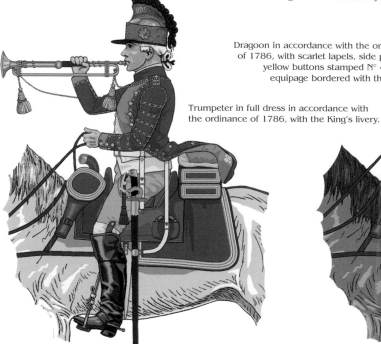

Trumpeter in full dress in accordance with the ordinance of 1786, with the King's livery.

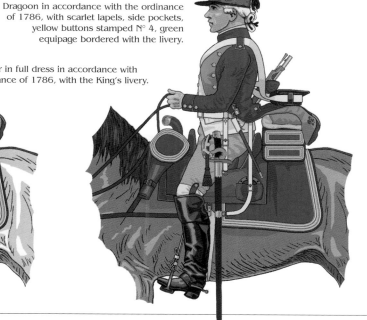

Dragoon in accordance with the ordinance of 1786, with scarlet lapels, side pockets, yellow buttons stamped N° 4, green equipage bordered with the livery.

for the royal regiments, except for the regiments of the Regimental hq, *La reine*, *Princes du Sang* and *gentilhommes*, who wore the livery of their commanding *Mestre-de-camp*.

Officers

Officers wore the same uniform as the troop made from Elbeuf serge, with golden or silver buttons, without any piping, stripes, buttonholes, or lace cuffs. The hat was decorated with black velvet, panache of feathers, but no plumage. The redingotes, coats and all of the equipment were identical to the Dragoons. They were recognizable by the absence of visors on their helmets that tilted towards the front. Each officer was armed with the same sabre, two pistols and a rifle with brass fittings. The saddle was covered with a shabrack in short skinned animal fur, with a band of serge in the same colour as the lapels on the edge. The saddlecloth was embroidered with a small gold or silver 33 mm stripe for the *Mestre-de-camp*, the lieutenant Colonel and the major, a 26 mm stripe for the captain, 22 mm for the lieutenant and 13 mm for the second lieutenant and the officers attached to headquarters. The officers could only wear their function even if they were superior in rank.

The commanding *Mestre-de-camp* wore a pleated gold or silver epaulette on each shoulder, depending on the colour of the buttons, decorated with fringes, knotted cords and gold and silver rolled knotted cords.

The second *Mestre-de-Camp* wore the same epaulettes as the commanding Mestre-de-camp with two flame-coloured cords running longwise through the centre.

The lieutenant-colonel wore the same epaulette as the commanding *Mestre-de-camp* on the left, and the same counter-epaulette on the right without any fringes.

The major wore a gold or silver epaulette on both sides decorated with fringes.

The commanding captain wore an epaulette on the left stipulated for the major and a counter-epaulette on the right.

The captain in second wore the same epaulette and a counter-epaulette, divided in the centre by a silk fire-coloured pleated cord.

The first lieutenant wore a chequered fire-coloured silk epaulette, fringes in gold, silver or silk.

The lieutenant in second wore the same epaulette as the first lieutenant, divided lengthwise by a silk flame–coloured cord.

The second lieutenant wore a silk fire-coloured epaulette with gold or silver squares and fringes in silk, gold or silver.

The quarter master treasurer wore the epaulette of a first or second lieutenant, depending on the rank to which he would be placed in the regiment.

The standard – bearer wore an epaulette with a silk flame-coloured background, bordered with gold or silver, and decorated with mixed fringes.

ORDINANCE FROM 21st FEBRUARY 1779

On January 29th 1779, the organisation of squadrons from the light cavalry, having not given full satisfaction, were withdrawn from the Dragoon regiments, forming six new regiments of Chasseurs à Cheval, placed thereafter in the Dragoons. The corps had 24 Dragoon regiments and 6 mounted chasseurs, all of them made up of 4 squadrons to a company of 70 men and mounted sub officers and 30 infantry, making a total of 400 men for each regiment, 280 of whom were mounted and 120 infantry, in all there were 12 000 men. On the following March 20th, all of the squadrons were modified again, with 80 Dragoons and mounted sub officers and 20 infantry, making 320 men on horseback and 80 infantry.

Uniform

The ordinance from 1776 was not greatly appreciated and was not completely applied. On February 21st 1779, a new royal ordinance, simplified the distribution of all of the regimental distinctive colours in order to recognize each other more easily in times of war. From this period, the distinctive colour was reproduced in the form of piping on the shoulder straps, the pocket turn backs and the facings.

All of the regiment except Artois were split into six classes depending on their years of service, defined by their distinctive colours that were distributed in the division of the two regiments. The first regiment of each division wore the colour on the lapels and facings and the second division regiment on the facings only.

— *1st class scarlet:* 1st division Colonel-général and *Mestre-de-Camp-Général*; 2nd division Royal and Du Roi; 3rd division La Reine and Dauphine.

— *2nd class dark pink:* 1st division Monsieur and Artois (the latter was exceptional with white lapels and a scarlet collar and facings) and the second division the Orléans and Chartres divisions.

— *3rd class chamois:* 1st division Condé and Bourbon; 2nd division Conti and Penthièvre.

— *4th class crimson:* 1st division Boufflers and Lorraine; 2nd division Montmorency and La Rochefoucauld.

— *5th class aurora:* 1st division Deux-Ponts and Durfort; 2nd division Ségur and Languedoc.

— *6th class white;* one division Noailles and Schomberg.

La Reine Dragons

Dragoon in accordance with the ordinance of 1776, with crimson facings and lapels, white collar, white buttons stamped N° 5, crimson equipage bordered with the Queen's livery.

Dragoon in accordance with the ordinance of 1779, with facings and lapels in the distinctive red colour, long pockets, white buttons stamped N°5, red equipage bordered with the livery.

Braid with the Queen's livery, white cordonnet on blue background.

Officer in redingote in accordance with the ordinance of 1776 and 1786.

Infantry Dragoon in accordance with the ordinance of 1776.

Dragoon in coat in accordance with the ordinance of 1779, with *Brandebourg* decorative pieces on the equipage's braid, interior facings in the distinctive colour.

The pocket turn backs, bordered and fastened with three large buttons, were either cut on the sides with yellow buttons for the first division, or longwise with white buttons for the second divisions. The facings, open on the exterior were bordered and decorated with four small buttons, two on the facings and two on the forearm. The shoulder straps were bordered with the opposite colour and fastened near to the right–hand collar. The ordinance did not give regulations about the presence of fleurs de lis on the tails. The two regiments from the headquarters were always recognizable by their buttonholes with aurora braid with a stripe in the same colour on the lapels and the facings for the Colonel-Général. The Colonel-Général regiment had a saddlecloth showing a trophy with five guidons grouped together, two of them in blue, two in red and one in white. The trophies of the *Mestre-de-camp* regiment were made up of three guidons bundled together, blue, red and white.

All of the outfits, equipage and horse tack were more or less those regulated in 1767 and 1776. The colours of the house were modified, the jacket was cut shorter and the outfit was cut tighter with longer tails.

The rank distinctions between officers and sub-officers were the same but sewn diagonally as regulated in the future ordnance of 1786.

Weapons

Weapons included a pistol à coffre and a rifle, model 1777, still in competition against the former systems.

The sabre model 1767, with demi-basket iron mount, still in service, was followed by the model of 1781 for the Dragoons with the same brass mount, a leather scabbard with brass decorative pieces and a straight blade. Conjunctly the cavalry and Dragoon sabre model 1779-1783 was used up to the Revolution. It had a fleuron (*fleur de lis*) mount in polished iron, a straight blade measuring 97.5 cm and a blackened leather scabbard decorated with brass. The same type of sabre, model 1783 was more commonly used with a copper mount.

After the model 1767, officers were provided with a battle ready sabre model 1782 with gold brass, blade measuring 89.3 cm and a scabbard with a chape and a locket with iron rings.

THE ORDINANCE FROM OCTOBER 1st 1786

Since January 18th 1780 each squadron had 91 Dragoons and mounted sub officers and just 9 infantrymen. The last ordinance of the *Ancien Régime* was published on October 1st 1786, it concerned uniform, equipment and organisation. The ordinance remained a referential guide for the arms during the Revolution

and the Empire up to 1812.

Each regiment was made up of four squadrons, of a company divided into two divisions, which were split into four sub divisions, each one with two squads. Headquarters included a commanding *Mestre-de-camp*, 1 *Mestre-de-camp* in second, 1 Lieutenant-colonel, 1 major, 1 guidon-bearer, 1 Adjutant, 1 surgeon-major, 1 chaplain, 1 *Maréchal-expert*, 1 saddler and 1 armourer. Each squadron had a commanding captain, 1 captain in second, 1 captain à la suite, 1 lieutenant, 1 lieutenant in second, 2 second lieutenants, 1 *cadet gentilhomme*, 1 *Maréchal-des-logis* in chief, 1 *Maréchal-des-logis* in second, 1 *Fourrier-écrivain*, 8 *brigadiers* (one per squad), 2 trumpeters, 1 frater, 1 farrier, 1 postmaster and 84 Dragoons, 8 of whom were *appointés*. The number of officers was the same in time of war as in time of peace.

The Royal ordinance of March 17th 1788, decreased again the number of Dragoon regiments, by including the regiments of Boufflers, Montmorency, Deux-Ponts, Durfort and Ségur into the corps of the *Chasseurs à Cheval* which had become a distinctive arm. As regards the Dragoons, there only remained the regiments of the Colonel Général, Mestre de Camp Général, Royal, Du Roi, La Reine, Dauphin, Monsieur, Artois, Orléans, Chartres, Condé, Bourbon, Conti, Penthièvre, Lorraine, Angoulême, Noailles and Schomberg. The responsibilities of the Colonel-generals, *Mestres-de-camp* generals and commissioner generals were abolished for the Dragoons as for the cavalry and the hussars. Consequently, the corps leaders took the title of colonel, maintaining the old names of the respective regiments. With the Revolution uprising, the Dragoons maintained the same organisation contrary to the infantry.

Uniform

The 1786 ordinance was a model of its kind, with detailed descriptions of all of the uniform previously regulated in 1779. The Dragoons'French-style outfit was in dark green cloth with the turn backs in serge or caddis in the each regiment's distinctive colour. The turn backs were decorated with a *fleur de lis* on the outside and a badge on the inside in green woollen serge.

From this period regiments were divided into six series of distinctive colours allocated on the lapels and the facings. These series were distributed among the regiments with the yellow buttons with the side pockets or the white buttons with the long pockets.

— *The 1st series scarlet:* Colonel-Général, lapels and facings, yellow button; Mestre-de-camp Général, lapels, yellow button; Royal, lapels and facings, yellow button; Du Roi, lapels, yellow

(continued on page 64)

La Reine Dragons

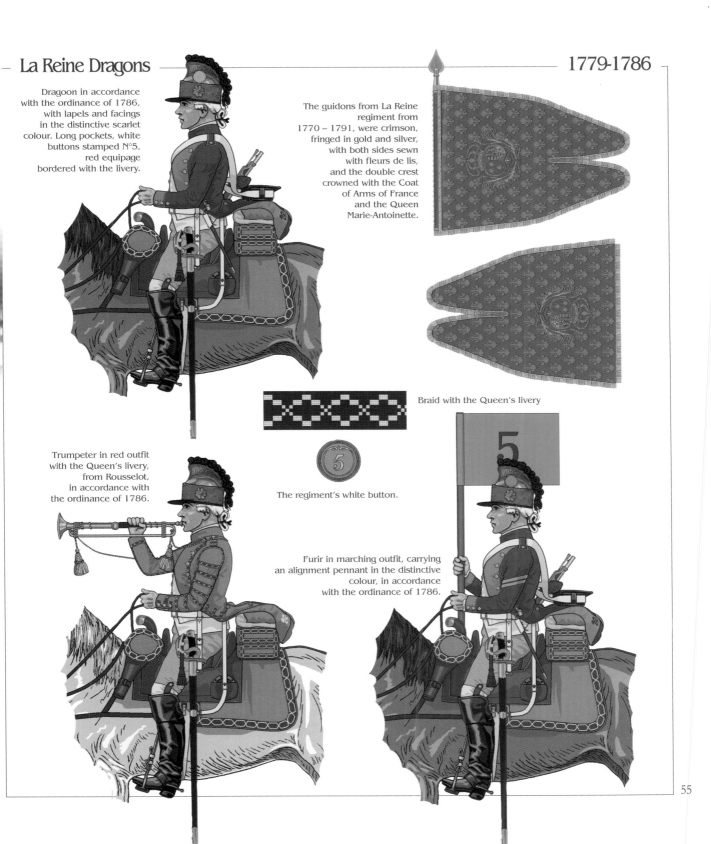

Dragoon in accordance with the ordinance of 1786, with lapels and facings in the distinctive scarlet colour. Long pockets, white buttons stamped N°5, red equipage bordered with the livery.

The guidons from La Reine regiment from 1770 – 1791, were crimson, fringed in gold and silver, with both sides sewn with fleurs de lis, and the double crest crowned with the Coat of Arms of France and the Queen Marie-Antoinette.

Braid with the Queen's livery

The regiment's white button.

Trumpeter in red outfit with the Queen's livery, from Rousselot, in accordance with the ordinance of 1786.

Furir in marching outfit, carrying an alignment pennant in the distinctive colour, in accordance with the ordinance of 1786.

55

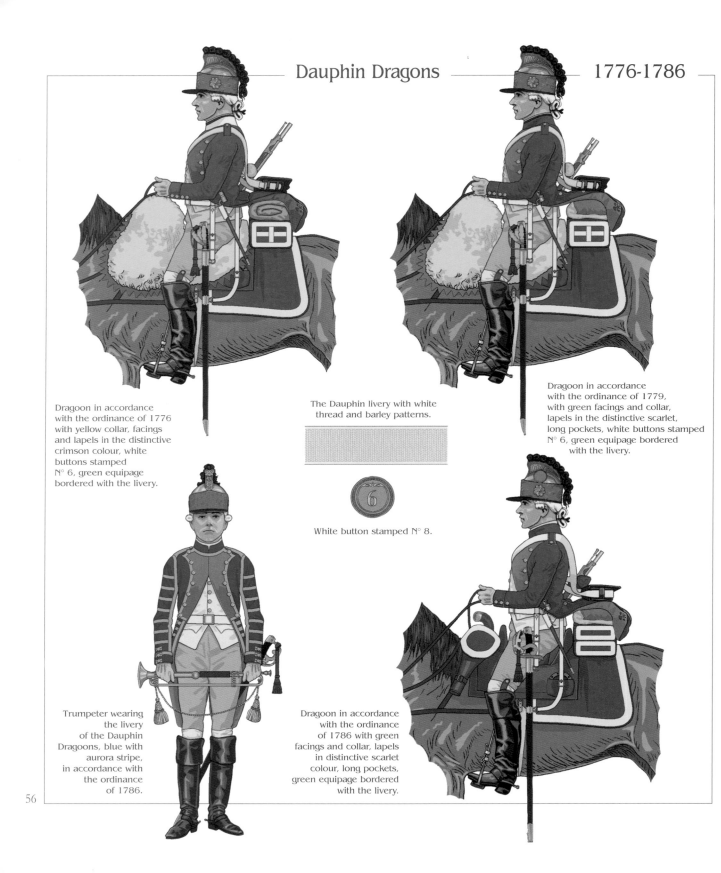

Dragoon in accordance with the ordinance of 1776 with yellow collar, facings and lapels in the distinctive crimson colour, white buttons stamped N° 6, green equipage bordered with the livery.

The Dauphin livery with white thread and barley patterns.

White button stamped N° 8.

Dragoon in accordance with the ordinance of 1779, with green facings and collar, lapels in the distinctive scarlet, long pockets, white buttons stamped N° 6, green equipage bordered with the livery.

Trumpeter wearing the livery of the Dauphin Dragoons, blue with aurora stripe, in accordance with the ordinance of 1786.

Dragoon in accordance with the ordinance of 1786 with green facings and collar, lapels in distinctive scarlet colour, long pockets, green equipage bordered with the livery.

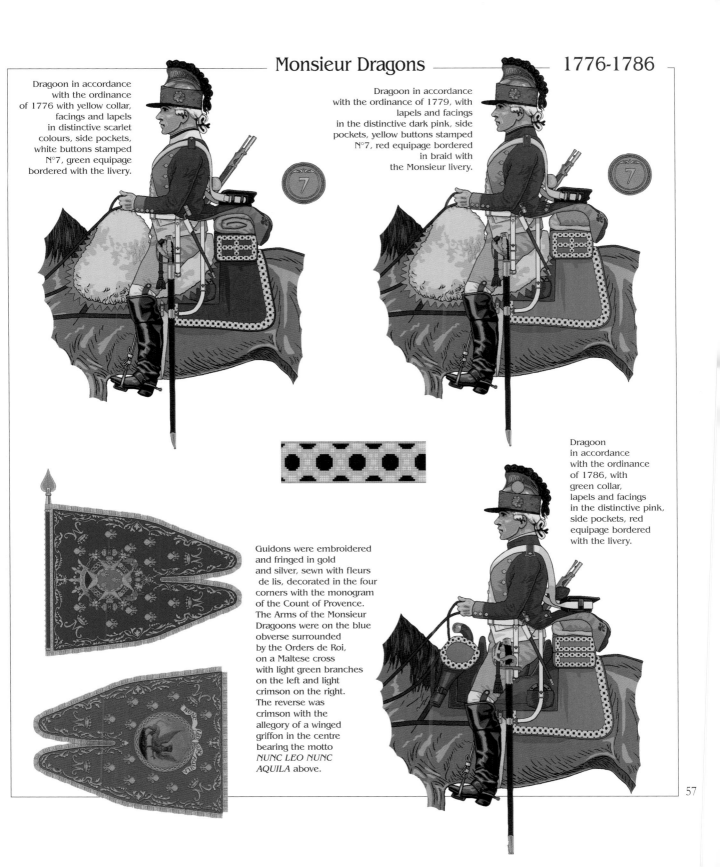

Dragoon in accordance with the ordinance of 1776 with yellow collar, facings and lapels in distinctive scarlet colours, side pockets, white buttons stamped N°7, green equipage bordered with the livery.

Dragoon in accordance with the ordinance of 1779, with lapels and facings in the distinctive dark pink, side pockets, yellow buttons stamped N°7, red equipage bordered in braid with the Monsieur livery.

Dragoon in accordance with the ordinance of 1786, with green collar, lapels and facings in the distinctive pink, side pockets, red equipage bordered with the livery.

Guidons were embroidered and fringed in gold and silver, sewn with fleurs de lis, decorated in the four corners with the monogram of the Count of Provence. The Arms of the Monsieur Dragoons were on the blue obverse surrounded by the Orders de Roi, on a Maltese cross with light green branches on the left and light crimson on the right. The reverse was crimson with the allegory of a winged griffon in the centre bearing the motto *NUNC LEO NUNC AQUILA* above.

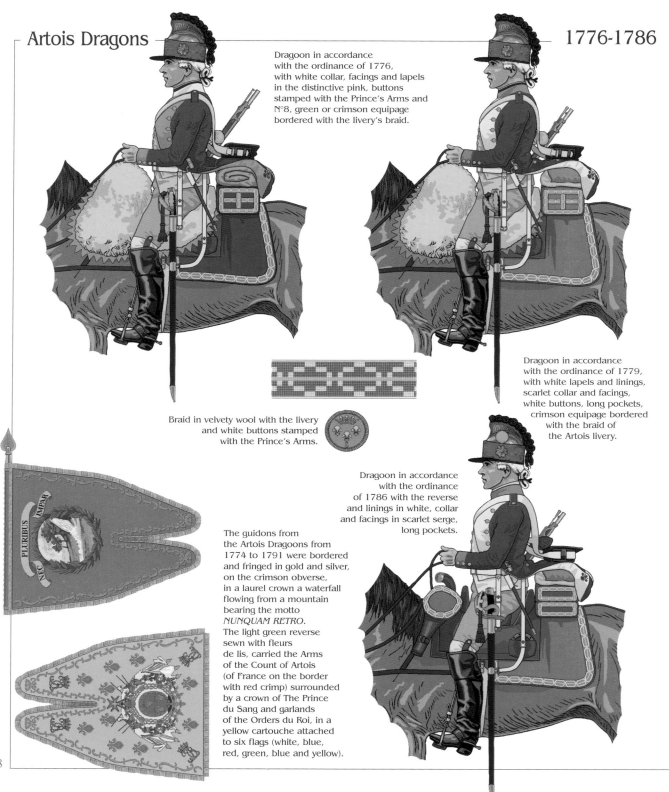

Dragoon in accordance
with the ordinance of 1776,
with white collar, facings and lapels
in the distinctive pink, buttons
stamped with the Prince's Arms and
N°8, green or crimson equipage
bordered with the livery's braid.

Dragoon in accordance
with the ordinance of 1779,
with white lapels and linings,
scarlet collar and facings,
white buttons, long pockets,
crimson equipage bordered
with the braid of
the Artois livery.

Braid in velvety wool with the livery
and white buttons stamped
with the Prince's Arms.

Dragoon in accordance
with the ordinance
of 1786 with the reverse
and linings in white, collar
and facings in scarlet serge,
long pockets.

The guidons from
the Artois Dragoons from
1774 to 1791 were bordered
and fringed in gold and silver,
on the crimson obverse,
in a laurel crown a waterfall
flowing from a mountain
bearing the motto
NUNQUAM RETRO.
The light green reverse
sewn with fleurs
de lis, carried the Arms
of the Count of Artois
(of France on the border
with red crimp) surrounded
by a crown of The Prince
du Sang and garlands
of the Orders du Roi, in a
yellow cartouche attached
to six flags (white, blue,
red, green, blue and yellow).

PLURIBUS IMPAR NEC

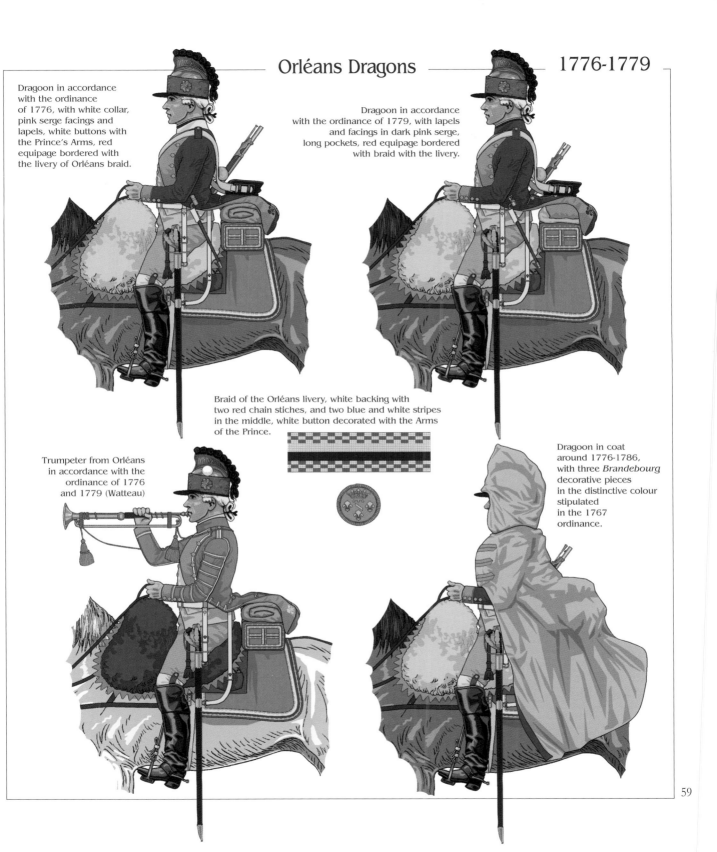

Orléans Dragons

Dragoon in accordance with the ordinance of 1776, with white collar, pink serge facings and lapels, white buttons with the Prince's Arms, red equipage bordered with the livery of Orléans braid.

Dragoon in accordance with the ordinance of 1779, with lapels and facings in dark pink serge, long pockets, red equipage bordered with braid with the livery.

Braid of the Orléans livery, white backing with two red chain stiches, and two blue and white stripes in the middle, white button decorated with the Arms of the Prince.

Trumpeter from Orléans in accordance with the ordinance of 1776 and 1779 (Watteau)

Dragoon in coat around 1776-1786, with three *Brandebourg* decorative pieces in the distinctive colour stipulated in the 1767 ordinance.

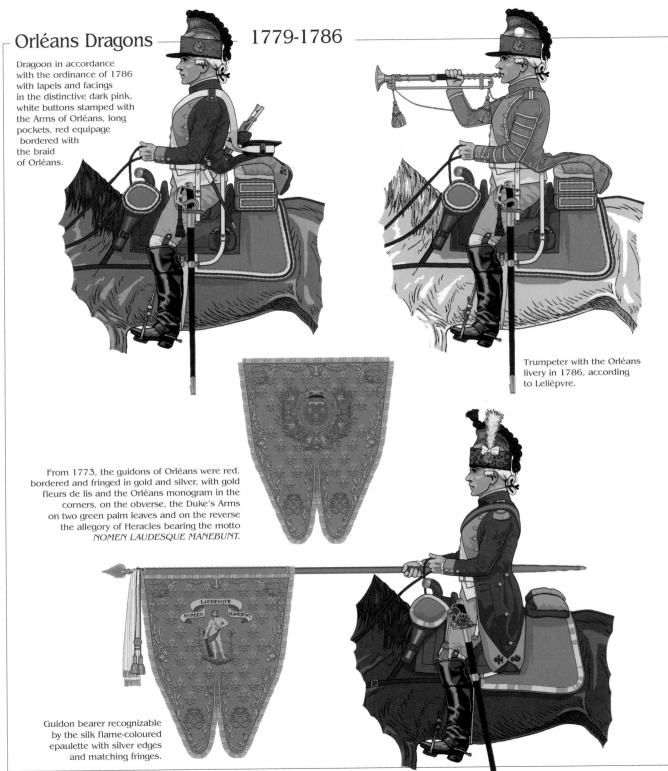

Orléans Dragons — 1779-1786

Dragoon in accordance
with the ordinance of 1786
with lapels and facings
in the distinctive dark pink,
white buttons stamped with
the Arms of Orléans, long
pockets, red equipage
bordered with
the braid
of Orléans.

Trumpeter with the Orléans
livery in 1786, according
to Lelièpvre.

From 1773, the guidons of Orléans were red,
bordered and fringed in gold and silver, with gold
fleurs de lis and the Orléans monogram in the
corners, on the obverse, the Duke's Arms
on two green palm leaves and on the reverse
the allegory of Heracles bearing the motto
NOMEN LAUDESQUE MANEBUNT.

Guidon bearer recognizable
by the silk flame-coloured
epaulette with silver edges
and matching fringes.

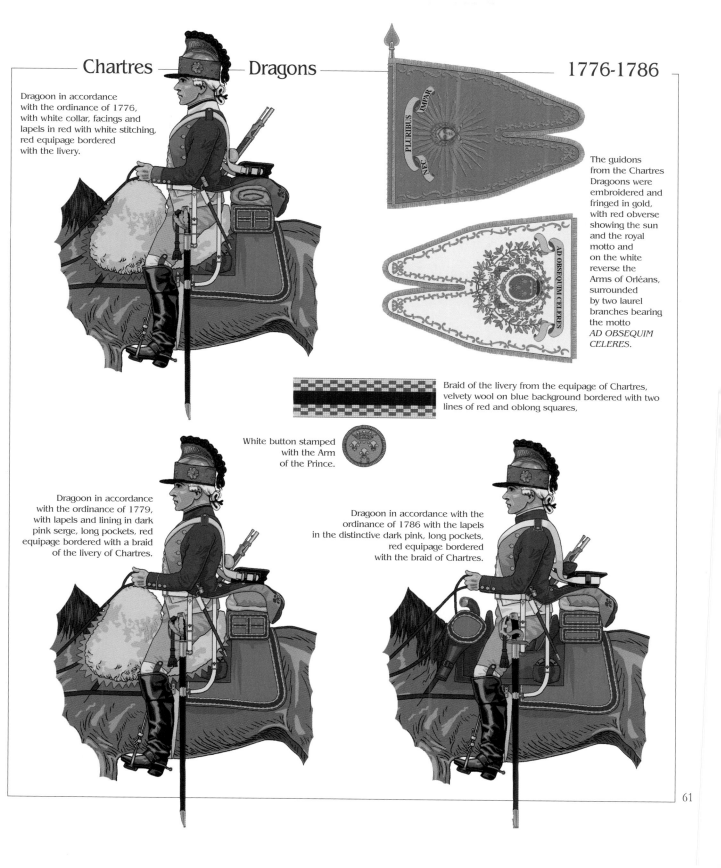

Chartres — Dragons — 1776-1786

Dragoon in accordance with the ordinance of 1776, with white collar, facings and lapels in red with white stitching, red equipage bordered with the livery.

The guidons from the Chartres Dragoons were embroidered and fringed in gold, with red obverse showing the sun and the royal motto and on the white reverse the Arms of Orléans, surrounded by two laurel branches bearing the motto *AD OBSEQUIM CELERES.*

Braid of the livery from the equipage of Chartres, velvety wool on blue background bordered with two lines of red and oblong squares,

White button stamped with the Arm of the Prince.

Dragoon in accordance with the ordinance of 1779, with lapels and lining in dark pink serge, long pockets, red equipage bordered with a braid of the livery of Chartres.

Dragoon in accordance with the ordinance of 1786 with the lapels in the distinctive dark pink, long pockets, red equipage bordered with the braid of Chartres.

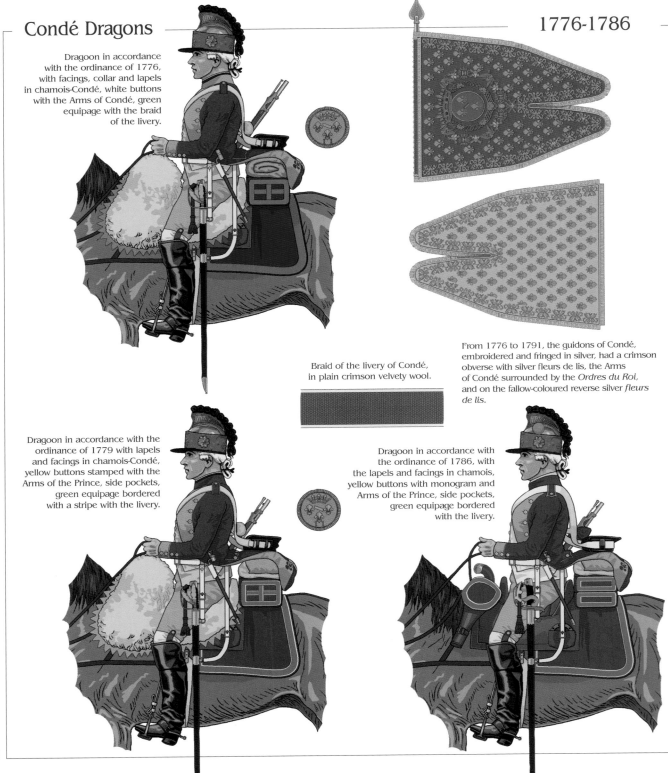

Condé Dragons

1776-1786

Dragoon in accordance
with the ordinance of 1776,
with facings, collar and lapels
in chamois-Condé, white buttons
with the Arms of Condé, green
equipage with the braid
of the livery.

Braid of the livery of Condé,
in plain crimson velvety wool.

From 1776 to 1791, the guidons of Condé,
embroidered and fringed in silver, had a crimson
obverse with silver fleurs de lis, the Arms
of Condé surrounded by the *Ordres du Roi*,
and on the fallow-coloured reverse silver *fleurs
de lis*.

Dragoon in accordance with the
ordinance of 1779 with lapels
and facings in chamois-Condé,
yellow buttons stamped with the
Arms of the Prince, side pockets,
green equipage bordered
with a stripe with the livery.

Dragoon in accordance with
the ordinance of 1786, with
the lapels and facings in chamois,
yellow buttons with monogram and
Arms of the Prince, side pockets,
green equipage bordered
with the livery.

62

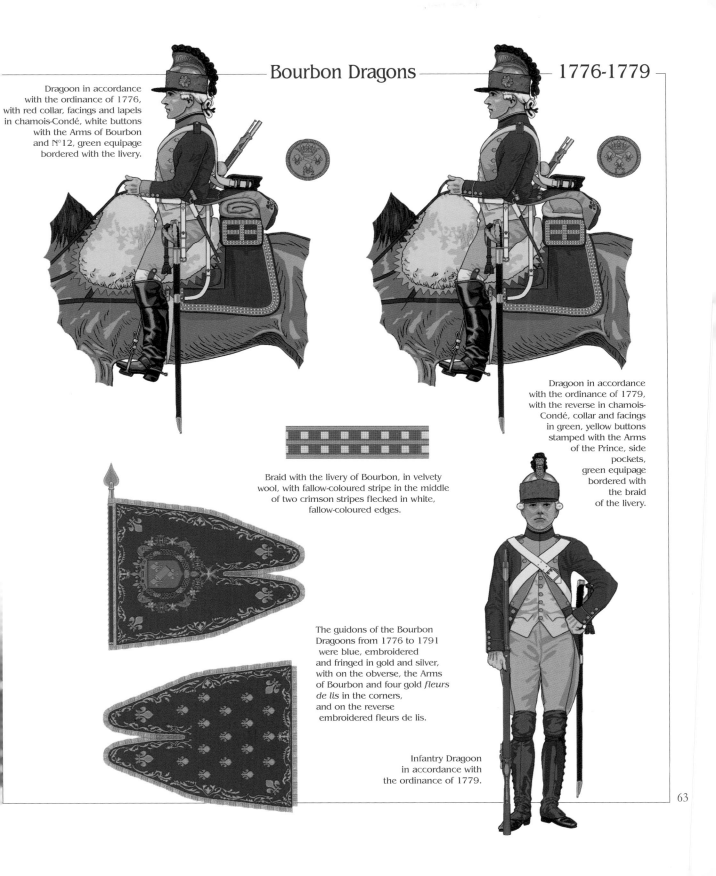

Bourbon Dragons ———— 1776-1779 —

Dragoon in accordance with the ordinance of 1776, with red collar, facings and lapels in chamois-Condé, white buttons with the Arms of Bourbon and N°12, green equipage bordered with the livery.

Braid with the livery of Bourbon, in velvety wool, with fallow-coloured stripe in the middle of two crimson stripes flecked in white, fallow-coloured edges.

Dragoon in accordance with the ordinance of 1779, with the reverse in chamois-Condé, collar and facings in green, yellow buttons stamped with the Arms of the Prince, side pockets, green equipage bordered with the braid of the livery.

The guidons of the Bourbon Dragoons from 1776 to 1791 were blue, embroidered and fringed in gold and silver, with on the obverse, the Arms of Bourbon and four gold *fleurs de lis* in the corners, and on the reverse embroidered fleurs de lis.

Infantry Dragoon in accordance with the ordinance of 1779.

63

button; La Reine, lapels, facings, white button; Dauphin, lapels, white button.

— *The 2nd series dark pink:* Monsieur, lapels and facings, yellow button; Artois white lapels, scarlet collar and facings, white button; Orléans, lapels and facings, white button; Chartres, lapels, white button.

— *The 3rd series chamois:* Condé, lapels and facings, yellow button; Bourbon, lapels, yellow button; Conti, lapels and facings, white button; Penthièvre, lapels, white button.

— *The 4th series crimson:* Boufflers, lapels and facings, yellow button; Lorraine, lapels, yellow button; Montmorency, lapels and facings, white button; La Rochefoucauld, lapels, white button.

— *The 5th series aurora:* Deux-Ponts, lapels and facings, yellow button; Durfort, lapels, yellow button; Ségur, lapels and facings, white button; Languedoc, lapels, white button.

— *The 6th series:* Noailles, lapels and facings, white button; Schomberg, lapels, white button.

The short jacket was in white woollen serge, lined in serge or white caddis, it fastened at the front with eight small buttons and two on each side of the pockets. The left pocket was imitation and the facings were round and decorated with two bone buttons.

The helmet remained the same, with a brass dome without any mouthpiece, a crest stamped with mouldings and palms on the sides and the head of Gorgona on the mask. The crest was decorated with a black or white frizzy mane for the Company *Colonelle* of the 1st regiment. Sometimes the front of the mane was attached with a kind of small crest. The shark skin turban was attached to the dome and it was fitted on each side with a rosette and eight small palm leaves in stamped copper. The adjustable visor in darkened leather fastened with five attachments. The only difference concerned the recognition of companies with a lentil-shaped crest, measuring a diameter of 45 mm placed above the left rosette.

It was wool in scarlet, sky blue, pink and marigold from the first to the fourth company, or white for the état-major, for the adjutants, the *maître-maréchal*, the saddler and the armourer. The Dragoons' horses were attached with a black ribbon tied in a rosette, with the two sides cut at the front.

The *pont-levis* culottes were in suede or sheepskin with five buttonholes at the opening.

The hooded coat in grey white serge flecked with blue was fitted with three *Brandebourg* braids allocated to the equipage of each regiment and decorated with serge or caddis on the front in the distinctive colour of the outfit. Two strips of material sewn into the seam around the waist meant that the coat or its pleats could be gathered onto the portmanteau.

The supple boots were in tough calfskin and were fitted with black iron spurs. The cuffs were in white wool and the gaiters in black linen, decorated with 24 leather buttons on each one, and a pair of garters.

Used outfits were made up of a surtout that was always cut in a scallop shape in dark green serge, fitted with eight large identical buttons, six of which were on the front buttonholes, one on top, two in the centre, and three at the bottom with the last two behind the hips. Two small buttons were placed next to the armhole to fasten the shoulder straps. The jacket was cut without tails in old serge.

The police bonnet was shaped into the Dragoon style in good quality green serge, lined with linen, bordered with a band of serge in the distinctive colour. The front was high cut and devoid of fittings and flames, it could be attached on the left side of the band, the top was decorated with a small crest in serge, cut from green and in the distinctive colour.

The small supplementary equipment belonging to the sub officers and the Dragoons consisted of three matelote shirts, without cuffs except for the *Maréchaux-des-logis* and the Furirs; two white collars lined with white linen and decorated with a brass buckle; a spare pair of skin culottes; two pairs of stockings; a pair of buckled shoes; a spare pair of boot cuffs and two handkerchiefs.

The shirts, gaiters and boot cuffs were all marked with the letter of each company. To help with their upkeep each man was provided with a powder bag and a crest to powder and all kinds of combs and brushes to fix, clean the outfit, boots and brass.

The equipment was made up of a *"Hungarian-style"* ceinturon belt, made from three white pieces of buffalo skin without any stitching, sewn onto two brass rings onto which were buttoned two sword hangers. A bayonet-holder was sewn onto the middle of the belt. The ceinturon was decorated with a curved brass buckle attached to two *ardillons* fixed at other end by a hook.

The *giberne* was in blackened stiff cow skin, it contained a elm or walnut wooden box, pierced in the centre with two lines of twelve holes and hollowed at the sides to fit a packet of fifteen cartridges and the white metal oil phial. On the other side of the flap which was cut with scalloped edges, was a blackened cow hide purse, to keep flint, oiled pieces and the bullet pliers.

The *giberne's* strap was in white buffalo skin, it was maintained in place by loops from the sides of the box and buckled underneath.

The strap was always decorated with buffalo skin, and fitted

(continued on page 72)

Bourbon — Dragons — 1779-1786

Lieutenant from the first
company in infantry
outfit in accordance
with the ordinance
of 1786.

Dragoon
in stable outfit
in accordance
with the
ordinance
of 1786
(Rousselot).

Dragoon in stable
outfit wearing long
culottes,
and a cream
woollen smock,
stipulated since
1776.

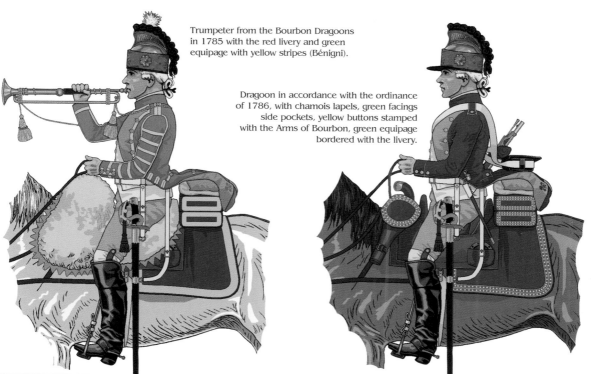

Trumpeter from the Bourbon Dragoons
in 1785 with the red livery and green
equipage with yellow stripes (Bénigni).

Dragoon in accordance with the ordinance
of 1786, with chamois lapels, green facings
side pockets, yellow buttons stamped
with the Arms of Bourbon, green equipage
bordered with the livery.

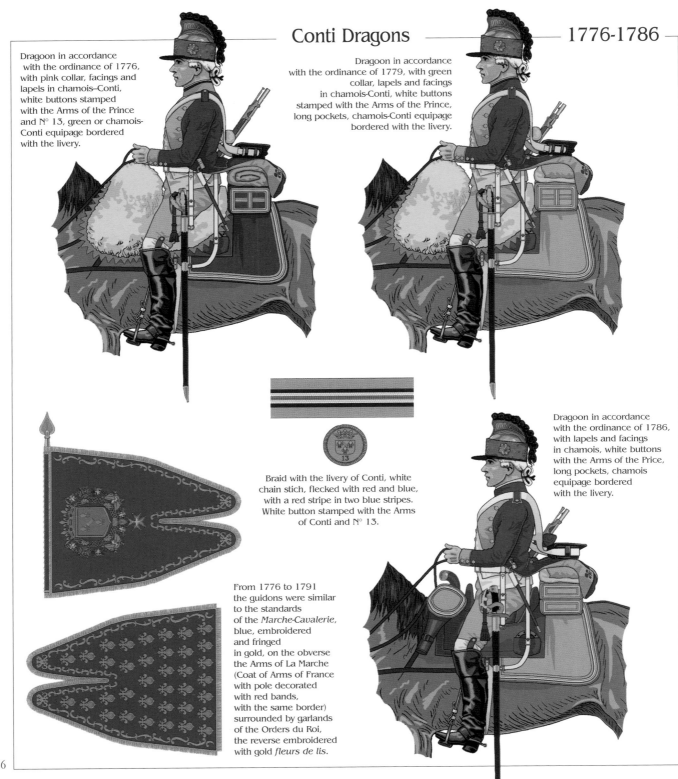

Conti Dragons

Dragoon in accordance with the ordinance of 1776, with pink collar, facings and lapels in chamois–Conti, white buttons stamped with the Arms of the Prince and N° 13, green or chamois-Conti equipage bordered with the livery.

Dragoon in accordance with the ordinance of 1779, with green collar, lapels and facings in chamois-Conti, white buttons stamped with the Arms of the Prince, long pockets, chamois-Conti equipage bordered with the livery.

Dragoon in accordance with the ordinance of 1786, with lapels and facings in chamois, white buttons with the Arms of the Price, long pockets, chamois equipage bordered with the livery.

Braid with the livery of Conti, white chain stich, flecked with red and blue, with a red stripe in two blue stripes. White button stamped with the Arms of Conti and N° 13.

From 1776 to 1791 the guidons were similar to the standards of the *Marche-Cavalerie*, blue, embroidered and fringed in gold, on the obverse the Arms of La Marche (Coat of Arms of France with pole decorated with red bands, with the same border) surrounded by garlands of the Orders du Roi, the reverse embroidered with gold *fleurs de lis*.

66

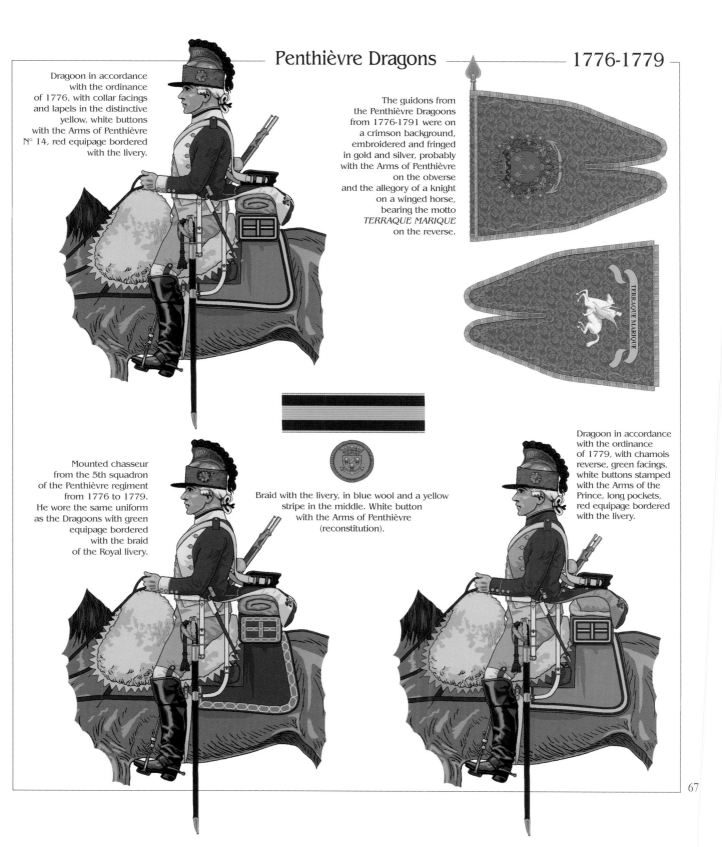

Penthièvre Dragons

Dragoon in accordance with the ordinance of 1776, with collar facings and lapels in the distinctive yellow, white buttons with the Arms of Penthièvre N° 14, red equipage bordered with the livery.

The guidons from the Penthièvre Dragoons from 1776-1791 were on a crimson background, embroidered and fringed in gold and silver, probably with the Arms of Penthièvre on the obverse and the allegory of a knight on a winged horse, bearing the motto *TERRAQUE MARIQUE* on the reverse.

TERRAQUE MARIQUE

Mounted chasseur from the 5th squadron of the Penthièvre regiment from 1776 to 1779. He wore the same uniform as the Dragoons with green equipage bordered with the braid of the Royal livery.

Braid with the livery, in blue wool and a yellow stripe in the middle. White button with the Arms of Penthièvre (reconstitution).

Dragoon in accordance with the ordinance of 1779, with chamois reverse, green facings, white buttons stamped with the Arms of the Prince, long pockets, red equipage bordered with the livery.

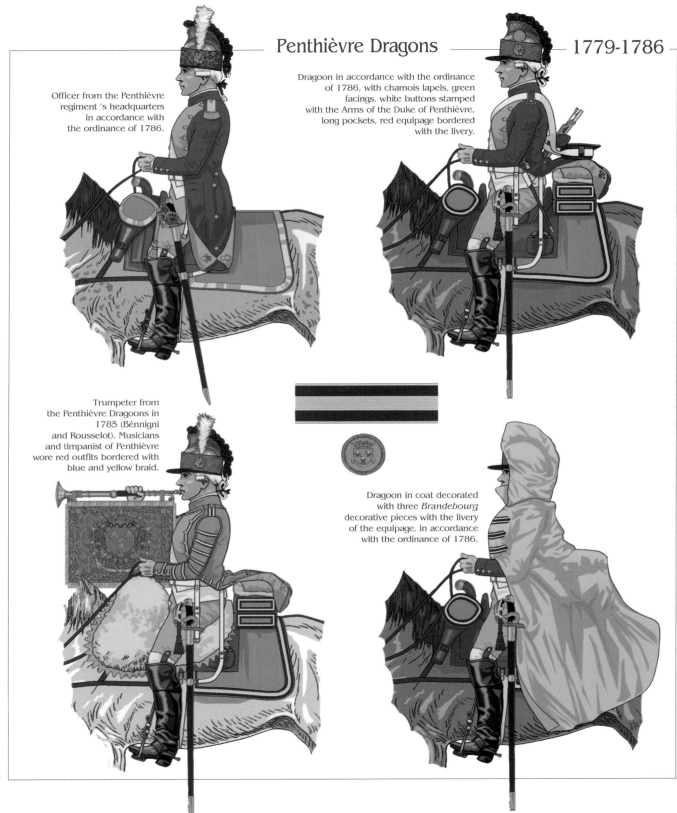

Officer from the Penthièvre regiment 's headquarters in accordance with the ordinance of 1786.

Dragoon in accordance with the ordinance of 1786, with chamois lapels, green facings, white buttons stamped with the Arms of the Duke of Penthièvre, long pockets, red equipage bordered with the livery.

Trumpeter from the Penthièvre Dragoons in 1785 (Bénnigni and Rousselot). Musicians and timpanist of Penthièvre wore red outfits bordered with blue and yellow braid.

Dragoon in coat decorated with three *Brandebourg* decorative pieces with the livery of the equipage, in accordance with the ordinance of 1786.

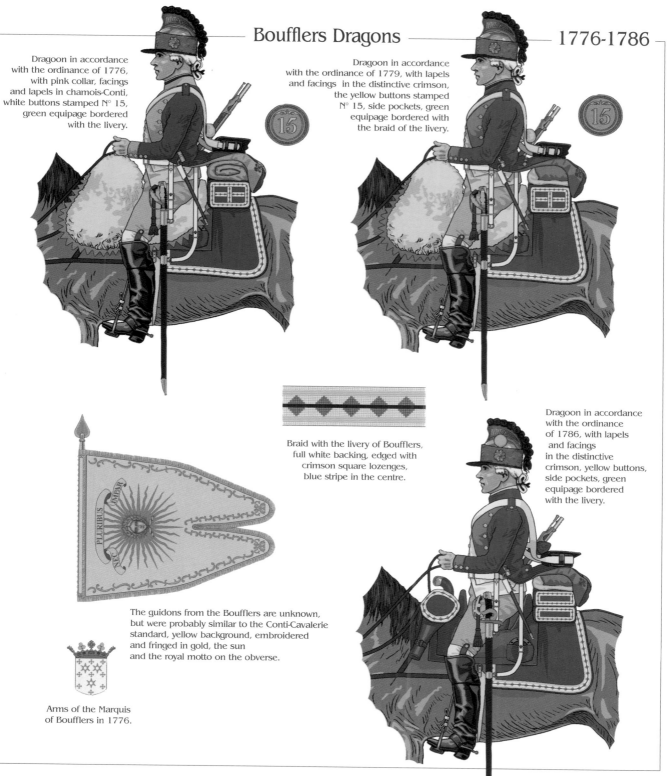

Boufflers Dragons

Dragoon in accordance with the ordinance of 1776, with pink collar, facings and lapels in chamois-Conti, white buttons stamped N° 15, green equipage bordered with the livery.

Dragoon in accordance with the ordinance of 1779, with lapels and facings in the distinctive crimson, the yellow buttons stamped N° 15, side pockets, green equipage bordered with the braid of the livery.

Braid with the livery of Boufflers, full white backing, edged with crimson square lozenges, blue stripe in the centre.

Dragoon in accordance with the ordinance of 1786, with lapels and facings in the distinctive crimson, yellow buttons, side pockets, green equipage bordered with the livery.

The guidons from the Boufflers are unknown, but were probably similar to the Conti-Cavalerie standard, yellow background, embroidered and fringed in gold, the sun and the royal motto on the obverse.

Arms of the Marquis of Boufflers in 1776.

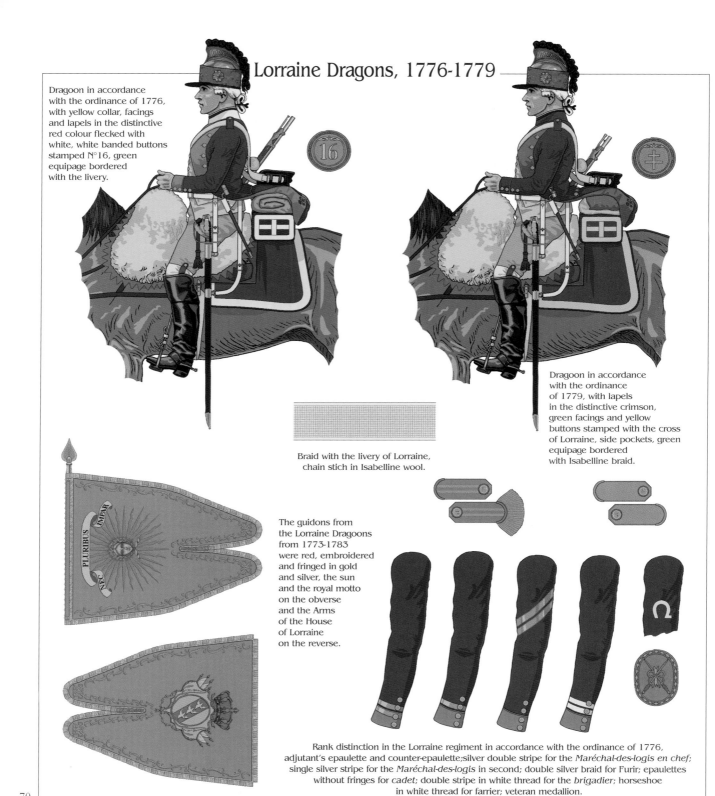

Lorraine Dragons, 1776-1779

Dragoon in accordance with the ordinance of 1776, with yellow collar, facings and lapels in the distinctive red colour flecked with white, white banded buttons stamped Nº16, green equipage bordered with the livery.

Dragoon in accordance with the ordinance of 1779, with lapels in the distinctive crimson, green facings and yellow buttons stamped with the cross of Lorraine, side pockets, green equipage bordered with Isabelline braid.

Braid with the livery of Lorraine, chain stich in Isabelline wool.

The guidons from the Lorraine Dragoons from 1773-1783 were red, embroidered and fringed in gold and silver, the sun and the royal motto on the obverse and the Arms of the House of Lorraine on the reverse.

Rank distinction in the Lorraine regiment in accordance with the ordinance of 1776, adjutant's epaulette and counter-epaulette;silver double stripe for the *Maréchal-des-logis en chef;* single silver stripe for the *Maréchal-des-logis* in second; double silver braid for Furir; epaulettes without fringes for *cadet;* double stripe in white thread for the *brigadier;* horseshoe in white thread for farrier; veteran medallion.

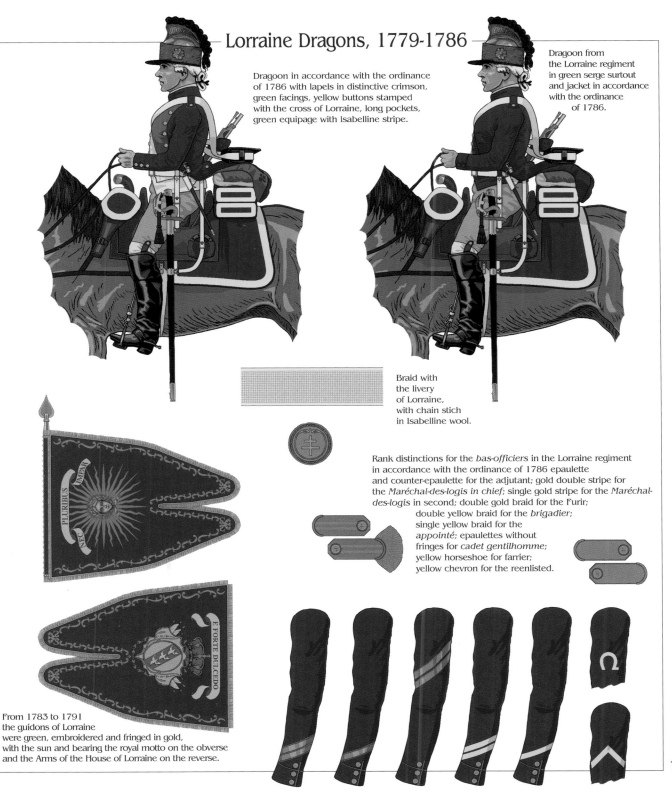

Lorraine Dragons, 1779-1786

Dragoon in accordance with the ordinance of 1786 with lapels in distinctive crimson, green facings, yellow buttons stamped with the cross of Lorraine, long pockets, green equipage with Isabelline stripe.

Dragoon from the Lorraine regiment in green serge surtout and jacket in accordance with the ordinance of 1786.

Braid with the livery of Lorraine, with chain stich in Isabelline wool.

Rank distinctions for the *bas-officiers* in the Lorraine regiment in accordance with the ordinance of 1786 epaulette and counter-epaulette for the adjutant; gold double stripe for the *Maréchal-des-logis in chief*; single gold stripe for the *Maréchal-des-logis in second*; double gold braid for the Furir; double yellow braid for the *brigadier*; single yellow braid for the *appointé*; epaulettes without fringes for *cadet gentilhomme*; yellow horseshoe for farrier; yellow chevron for the reenlisted.

From 1783 to 1791 the guidons of Lorraine were green, embroidered and fringed in gold, with the sun and bearing the royal motto on the obverse and the Arms of the House of Lorraine on the reverse.

71

with two additional straps with brass buckles to attach the bonnet.

Weapons

Infantry Dragoons were armed with just a rifle with its bayonet. The ordinance of 1786 did not change the Dragoons' weapons, maintaining the rifle and pistol à coffre model 1777 and the fleuron sabre model 1783 or the older model with demi-basket mount.

Equipage and horse tack

The saddlecloth was in serge in the colour attributed to the equipage of the horse, lined in cream linen and bordered with the livery stripe, 40 mm in width. The first two regiments maintained their trophies sewn onto the angle of the saddlecloth. The semi-oval shaped chaperon sewn to the font was in the same serge as the saddlecloth, bordered with the same stripe, lined in calf skin. Above the font was a leather pocket to protect the pistol.

The woollen portmanteau was in the colour attributed to the equipage, edged with 20 mm stripe of the livery. The coat was attached above it by three straps sewn into the inferior part of the portmanteau. The extremities were fitted from the inside with a piece of tough leather to give it more strength. This case contained all of the small equipment, as well as the jacket, the spare animal skin culottes, and enough bread for four days, as well as material to groom the horse.

The saddle and all of its equipment, including the bridle, the bites, the bridle's headstall and the snaffle in use by the regiment were in compliance with the previous description. The Dragoons' horses were smaller than those in the cavalry, measured 1,46 m to 1,51 m, all of them were marked with the corps number on their left buttock.

Bas-officiers (sub-officers or NCOs)

The sub officers from the regiments of the Regimental hq wore the distinctive stripes described below, in fine gold braid or yellow wool. All of the distinctions of ranks and functions were sewn onto the surtouts, and were under the responsibility of the sub officers and the Dragoons. The Adjutants, Maréchaux-des-logis, Furirs, brigadiers and trumpet players or drummers were armed with a sabre and just one pistol.

Only the Maréchaux-des-logis and the Furirs were allowed to wear shirt cuffs.

- The Adjutant wore an epaulette in a fire coloured silk backing, with two cords braided in gold or silver running lengthwise, fringes mixed with metal and fire coloured felt. An identical counter-epaulette without fringes on the right.

The Maréchal-des-logis in chief wore on the exterior of his forearm, two fine gold or silver 22 mm stripes, sewn diagonally from one sleeve seam to another.

The Maréchal-des-logis wore one gold or silver 22 mm stripes on his forearm above the facings.

The Furir having the rank of Maréchal-des-logis wore two gold or silver 22 mm stripes, sewn across the sleeve, above the fold in the two arms. For the encampment or on horseback, he carried a long white pole measuring 2 m with a banner (distinguishing flag) in serge in the distinctive regimental colours, carrying the number of the opposite colour.

The brigadier wore two white or yellow 22 mm stripes sewn diagonally on the outside of the forearm, sewn from one sleeve seam to another.

The appointee wore just one white or yellow 22 mm stripes, in the same place as the brigadier.

The cadet gentilhomme wore two epaulettes without fringes, with gold or silver 33 mm stripes, lined and edged in the distinctive colour serge.

The farrier wore on his sleeves above the arm folds, a horseshoe stripes in white or yellow thread, 22 mm in width.

The reenlisted, as in 1771 (picture 57).

The trumpet players and drummers, wore the blue outfit with the King's livery with the lapels, facings, jacket, culottes and linings in the distinctive colours. The pockets were cut and placed in accordance with each regiment's regulations. The regiments of the Regimental hq, La Reine, Princes du Sang and Gentilhommes continued to wear the outfit with the livery of their commanding Mestres-de-camp, with the distinctive regimental colours. The stripes with the livery and other decorations remained the same and were allocated in the same order as for the infantry. The Dragoons' drum box's strap was similar to the infantry's. The trumpet players were under the authority of the most experienced, having the rank of appointé. There were four drummers in times of peace and six in times of war. From 1788 the rank of Drum–major was given to all of the regiments. The musicians wore the same outfit as the trumpet players and the drummers, but without the livery.

Officers

The ordinance did not make any changes, only the helmet was replaced by the cavalry hat for off duty service. It was fitted with a cockade, and a goat's hair crest in the colour attributed to the company. The helmet remained without visor, and the horses were attached by the tail rather than

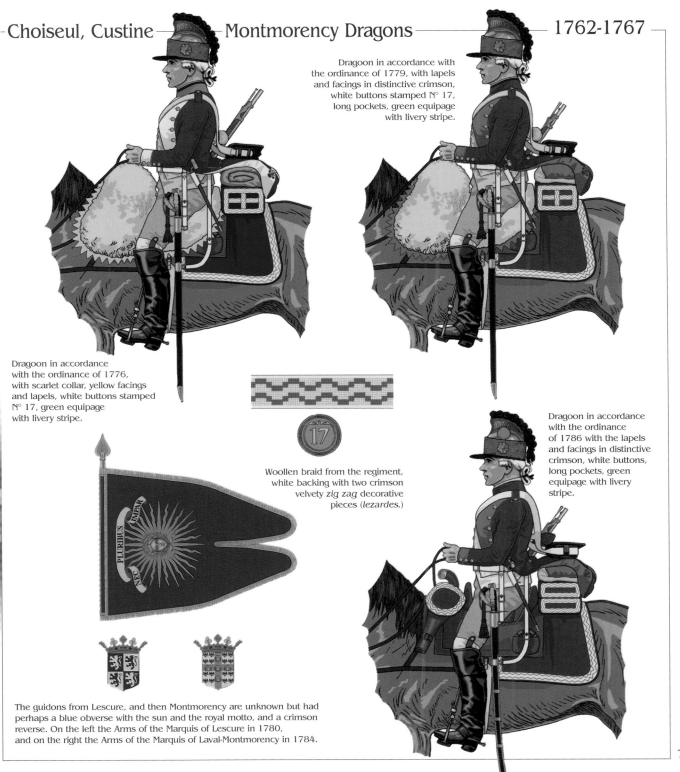

Dragoon in accordance with the ordinance of 1779, with lapels and facings in distinctive crimson, white buttons stamped N° 17, long pockets, green equipage with livery stripe.

Dragoon in accordance with the ordinance of 1776, with scarlet collar, yellow facings and lapels, white buttons stamped N° 17, green equipage with livery stripe.

Woollen braid from the regiment, white backing with two crimson velvety *zig zag* decorative pieces (*lezardes.*)

PLURIBUS IMPAR NEC

Dragoon in accordance with the ordinance of 1786 with the lapels and facings in distinctive crimson, white buttons, long pockets, green equipage with livery stripe.

The guidons from Lescure, and then Montmorency are unknown but had perhaps a blue obverse with the sun and the royal motto, and a crimson reverse. On the left the Arms of the Marquis of Lescure in 1780, and on the right the Arms of the Marquis of Laval-Montmorency in 1784.

with bows. The coat was in green serge with collar edged with a gold or silver stripes, and faced with the distinctive colours. The *rotonde* redingote was abolished in 1779, came back into use in times of peace only. The *ceinturon* belt in white buffalo was identical to the Dragoons, it was worn over the jacket. The boots were the same as the troops'with spurs in bronzed iron.

The saddle was the colour of the saddlecloth, with bridle's bites decorated with small yellow bumps, stamped similar to the outfit's buttons.

The saddlecloths and the chaperons were in serge, and in the same colour as the regimental colour, edged with a gold or silver 66 mm stripe for the *Mestres-de-camp*, Lieutenant–Colonels and Majors, a 53 mm stripe for the captains, a 44 mm stripe for the Lieutenants and a 33 mm stripe for the second-Lieutenants and other officers attached to the Regimental hq. All of the fittings, fringes, coat of arms and any other decorative pieces on the equipage were forbidden.

Each officer was armed with two pistols, a sabre with a fire – coloured strap or cord mixed with gold thread and silk, identical to the epaulettes. Off duty the officers carried a sword *"à la mousquetaire"* regulated for the infantry with the *ceinturon* belt worn over the jacket or around the neck, held in place by a counter-epaulette, as in the infantry.

Officers could only wear stripes showing their functional rank, even if they were superior in rank. The officers'ranks were regulated in 1776, with for the new ranks of captain and second Lieutenant, an epaulette split down the middle by two fire–coloured cords.

Guidons

According to the *Etats Militaires* of 1748, only one guidon was used as a rallying point in a Dragoon squadron. This usage was generalised throughout the cavalry in an ordinance dated 1762. Since 1753, the guard of the guidons was confided to a brigadier and 12 Dragoons placed at the head of the 1st company of the 1st squadron. During combat, the guidons remained at the back with the mounted soldiers. The salute to the royal white guidon by the Colonel General was done with upturned rifles, bayonet in the muskets.

The ordinance of March 25th 1776 stated that each regiment should have no more than two guidons, each one entrusted to a guidon-bearer, second Lieutenant or alternatively a Maréchal-des-logis. The guidon was placed in 2nd rank of the 2nd squadron's company, in the 3rd left line. This decision was contradicted in the ordinance of July 25th 1784, that provided a guidon for each of the four squadrons, attached to the 1st company.

The guidons were made from tough damask silk, known as *"de gros tours"* double thickness, sewn with fringes. The fabric was royal blue for the royal regiments or the different colours of livery, or the distinctive regimental colours of princes and *gentilhommes*. The fringes were in gold or silver for the Royal and Princes du sang regiments, or gold for the gentilhomme regiments. The guidon dimensions were approximately 80 to 100 cm high and 95 to 125 cm long, with the tendency to reduce their size towards the end of the regime.

On the obverse there was usually the great King's sun shining, embroidered in gold, with His Majesty's motto above *NEC PLURIBUS IMPAR*, in black on a silver border. The reverse differs by its allegories, heraldry, coat of arms with sentences proper to the House of its proprietors.

The Royal guidons or the Prince guidons were commonly sewn with fleurs de lis, dolphins, or gold or silver flames on both sides. Gradually the guidons became simpler, among others the disappearance of embroidered edges.

The pole was originally shaped like a *"lance for tournois"*, but it was modified and it became a pole without its handle, another was a second model known as *"à baguettes"* made from iron rods pined along the sides of the wood up to the fabric, to protect from blows from sabres. On this pole model, the diameter was 25 mm at the bottom, 45 mm at the most, with a 20 cm handle covered with velvet or suede, with a triangular iron ring holder. The lower extremity of the pole was reinforced with a polished iron foot and the tip was decorated with a gilded tip sometimes sculptured with fleurs de lis.

The poles were generally painted in blue for the royal regiments or in the fabric colour for the other regiments. On horseback the pole's foot rested on a leather patch attached to the right hand side of the stirrups, and held in place by a snap hook attached to the triangle's strap.

The strap was beautifully decorated in the princes'regiments in a natural buffalo skin, edged with the gold or silver stripe with a rifle holster. The fabric was fitted to the pole by sixty gilded round-headed nails the length of a stripe.

Since the Battle of Fleurus all of the regiments carried on campaign, the white flag, generally without fringes, held in place by gold or silver silk bullion cords.

During marches the guidons were rolled and put into a fawn or black leather sliding holder known as a "bourse". The poles, flags and holders were under the responsibility of the Mestre-de-camp proprietors, they were renewed every 18 to 20 years, even though the fabric was supplied by the King.

We do not know a lot about the guidons and standards from the ancienne monarchie, due to the public burning during the Revolution.

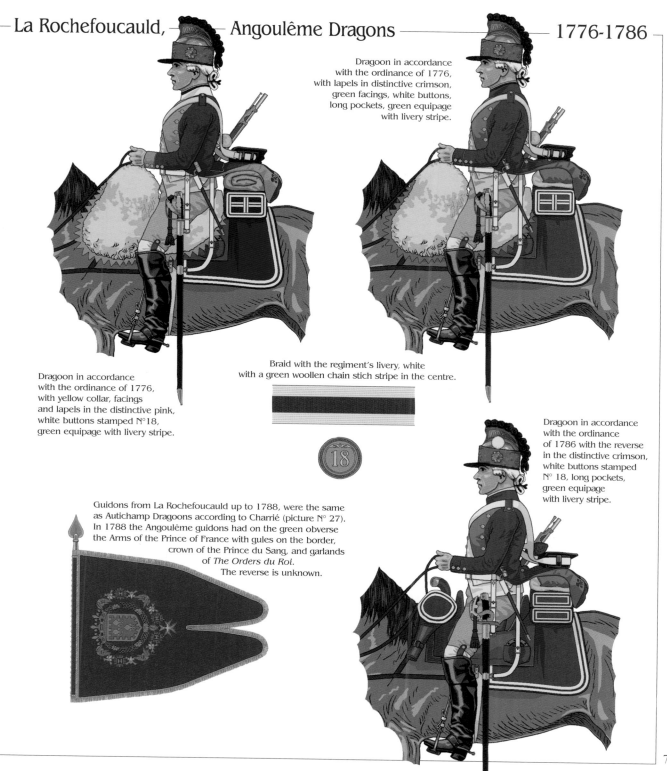

Dragoon in accordance
with the ordinance of 1776,
with lapels in distinctive crimson,
green facings, white buttons,
long pockets, green equipage
with livery stripe.

Dragoon in accordance
with the ordinance of 1776,
with yellow collar, facings
and lapels in the distinctive pink,
white buttons stamped N°18,
green equipage with livery stripe.

Braid with the regiment's livery, white
with a green woollen chain stich stripe in the centre.

Dragoon in accordance
with the ordinance
of 1786 with the reverse
in the distinctive crimson,
white buttons stamped
N° 18, long pockets,
green equipage
with livery stripe.

Guidons from La Rochefoucauld up to 1788, were the same
as Autichamp Dragoons according to Charrié (picture N° 27).
In 1788 the Angoulême guidons had on the green obverse
the Arms of the Prince of France with gules on the border,
crown of the Prince du Sang, and garlands
of *The Orders du Roi*.
The reverse is unknown.

REGIMENTAL HISTORY, 1776

1st rank. Colonel Général Dragoons (royal)

Regiment created and commanded by the Colonel-Général of the Dragoons on April 2nd 1668, for the Count of Péquilain (future Duke of Lauzun). It was comprised of companies from the *Étrangers du Roi* Dragoons Regiment, and ranked first in its arm. In 1714, the Conflans Regiment was included into its ranks.

From 1776 to 1779, the first and second Chasseurs companies from the *Légion Royale* formed a fifth squadron. In 1791, the former Colonel-Général, became the fifth Dragoon Regiment. *(Pages 5, 23, 46)*

2nd rank. Mestre-de-Camp Général Dragoons (royal)

Regiment created following the purchase of the Count of Quincy's carabins, by the Count of Tessé on March 25th 1674, placed 7th in rank in the Dragoons. On December 17th 1684, Tessé took command of the Mestre de camp général Dragoons, ranked 2nd in its arm. In 1713 and in 1714, the Bellisle regiments and part of the Conflans regiments were included into its ranks.

From 1776 to 1779, the 3rd and 4th companies from the Légion Royale chasseurs formed a 5th squadron.

In 1791, the former Mestre-de-Camp Général became the 10th Dragoon Regiment. *(Pages 7, 25, 47)*

3rd rank Royal Dragoons (royal)

Regiment created in 1668, ranked 3rd in its arm, known as the Royal Dragoons. It was comprised of companies that came from the *Étrangers du Roy* and Colonel Général Dragoon regiments. In 1713 and 1714, the Houdetot regiment and part of the Bouville regiment were included into its ranks.

From 1776 to 1779, the 5th and 6th companies from the Légion Royale Chasseurs formed a 5th squadron. In 1791, the former Royal-Dragoons became the 1st Dragoon Regiment. *(Pages 8, 28, 48, 50)*

4th rank Du Roi Dragoons (royal)

Regiment created on January 24th 1744, known as the Du Roi Dragoons and placed 4th in rank in its arm. It was comprised of companies taken from all of the 15 Dragoon regiments. From 1776 to 1779, the 7th and 8th companies

from the Légion Royale Chasseurs formed the 5th squadron. In 1791, the former Du Roi became the 18th Dragoon Regiment. *(Pages 9, 10, 29, 50, 51)*

5th rank La Reine Dragoons (royal)

This regiment was created on September 14th 1673 by the Chevalier of Hocquincourt with companies taken from the Colonel Général and the Royal Dragoons.

On July 31st 1675, the regiment was bought by the *Maison Royale*, and given the title of La Reine Dragoons and ranked 4th in the arm. Between 1713 and 1714, regiments from the Lande, Saint-Sernin de Rohan-Chabot were included.

In 1744, the regiment was ranked 5th in the arm. From 1776 to 1779, the 1st and 2nd companies from the Légion de Flandre Chasseurs formed a 5th squadron.

In 1791, the former Reine became the 6th Dragoon Regiment. *(Pages 11, 30, 53, 55)*

6th rank Dauphin Dragoons (royal)

Regiment created on September 24th 1673, and ranked as 4th in the arm. In August 1675, the regiment was given the title of the Dauphin Dragoons in honour of the King's eldest son. The regiment was placed 5th in rank in 1675, and then 6th in rank in 1750.

In 1714, the Bretagne Regiment was included into its ranks. From 1776 to 1779 the 3rd and 4th companies from the Légion de Flandres Chasseurs formed a 5th squadron. In 1791, the former Dauphin became the 7th Dragoon regiment. *(Pages 13, 31, 56)*

7th rank Monsieur Dragoons (prince)

Regiment created in the Languedoc, by the Marquis of Barbezières on October 4th 1676, placed 13th in rank, and the 7th in 1724, known under the name of its successive Mestres de camp and proprietors (1676 Barbezières, 1678 Firmaçon, 1710 Foix, 1713 Chatillon, 1714 Gœsbriant, 1724 Condé-Bourbon, 1740 Mailly, 1744 Egmont, 1753 Marbeuf, 1761 Chabrillan, 1763 Monteclerc, 1774 Monsieur).

In 1713, the Parpailles and Sevron Regiments were included into its ranks. On December 12th 1724, the

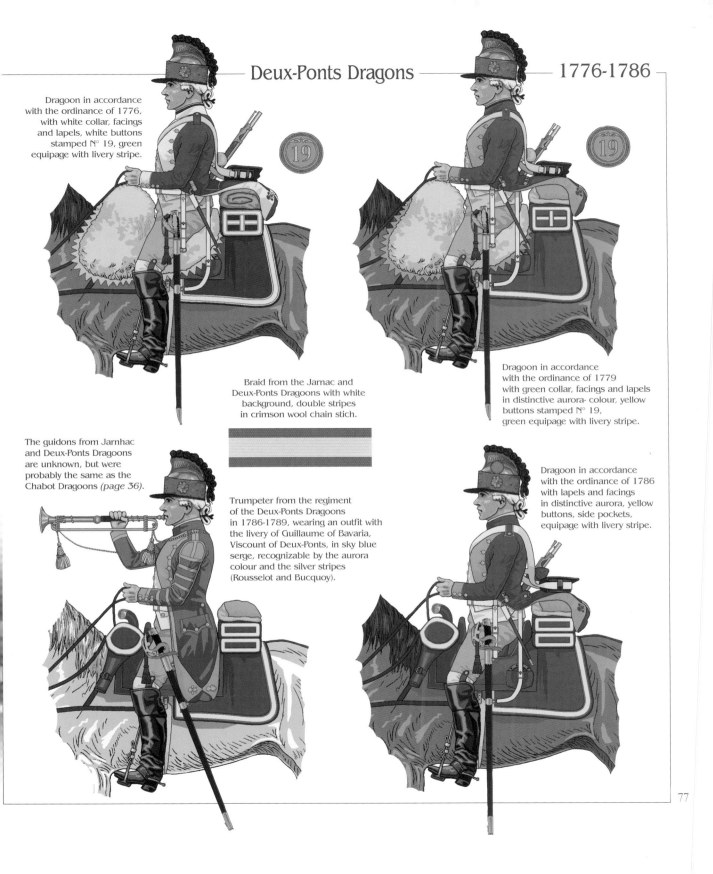

Dragoon in accordance with the ordinance of 1776, with white collar, facings and lapels, white buttons stamped N° 19, green equipage with livery stripe.

Braid from the Jarnac and Deux-Ponts Dragoons with white background, double stripes in crimson wool chain stich.

The guidons from Jarnhac and Deux-Ponts Dragoons are unknown, but were probably the same as the Chabot Dragoons (page 36).

Trumpeter from the regiment of the Deux-Ponts Dragoons in 1786-1789, wearing an outfit with the livery of Guillaume of Bavaria, Viscount of Deux-Ponts, in sky blue serge, recognizable by the aurora colour and the silver stripes (Rousselot and Bucquoy).

Dragoon in accordance with the ordinance of 1779 with green collar, facings and lapels in distinctive aurora- colour, yellow buttons stamped N° 19, green equipage with livery stripe.

Dragoon in accordance with the ordinance of 1786 with lapels and facings in distinctive aurora, yellow buttons, side pockets, equipage with livery stripe.

regiment became under the ownership of the Prince of Condé Duke of Bourbon and of Enghien.

The regiment was demoted to 15th rank in 1740 and then to 7th rank in 1776. On February 21st 1774, the regiment took the name of the Count of Province (future Louis XVIII), and was renamed Monsieur Dragoons on May 10th 1774, following the death of Louis XV.

From 1776 to 1779, the 5th and 6th companies from the Légion de Flandre Chasseurs formed a 5th squadron.

In 1791, the former Monsieur became the 13th Dragoon Regiment. *(Pages 22, 43, 57)*

8th rank Artois Dragoons (prince)

Regiment created on February 5th 1675, following the amalgam of the Franches and Liégeoises companies, and placed 8th in rank and then 12th in rank in its arm, under the name of its successive Mestres de camp, (1675 La Bretesche, 1682 Chevilly, 1688 Caylus, 1696 Lautrec, 1720 Rochepierre, 1728 Harcourt, 1743 Lillebonne-Harcourt, 1748 Harcourt, 1758 Flamarins, 1762 Coigny, 1765 Damas, 1767 Thianges, 1774 Artois).

In 1714, Saint-Chamond Regiment was included into its ranks. On May 20th 1774, the regiment was owned by the Count of Artois (future Charles X). From 1776 to 1779, the 7th and 8th companies from the Légion de Flandre Chasseurs formed a 5th squadron. In 1776, Artois Dragoons, was demoted to 8th rank, and received the 4th squadron from the Légion de Flandre Chasseurs. In 1791, the former Artois became the 12th Dragoon Regiment *(Pages 19, 37, 58)*

9th rank Orléans Dragoons (prince)

Regiment made up from the Franches companies, for the Regent on April 1st 1718, known under the name of the Orléans Dragoons.

The regiment was placed 6th in rank in 1733, then 7th in 1744, and 9th in 1776. From 1776 to 1779, the 1st and 2nd companies from the Légion de Lorraine Chasseurs formed a 5th squadron.

In 1788, the regiment was reorganised, in 1791 it became the 16th Dragoon Regiment. *(Pages 14, 32, 59, 60)*

10th rank Chartres Dragoons (prince)

Regiment created on March 3rd 1672, by the Marquis de Seyssac and placed 48th in rank in the cavalry, known under the name of its successive gentilhomme, Mestres de camp and proprietors (1672 Seyssac, 1676 Imécourt, 1702

Montauban, 1703 Forbin, 1708 Chépy, 1744 Bellefonds). In 1757, the regiment was demoted to 47th rank in its arm. On May 7th 1758, it was owned by the Prince of Chartres, known under the name of Chartres-Cavalry under the command of a Mestre de camp-lieutenant.

In 1762, Chartres was demoted to 25th rank in its arm, and the former Trasegnies-Cavalry was promoted to 39th rank. In accordance with the ordinance of March 25th 1776, Chartres was transferred to 10th rank in the Dragoons arm. From 1776 to 1779, the 3rd and 4th companies from the Légion de Lorraine Chasseurs formed a 5th squadron. In 1791, the former Chartres became the 14th Dragoon Regiment. *(Page 61)*

11th rank Condé Dragoons (prince)

Regiment from the House of Princes of Condé, became a cavalry regiment on May 16th 1635, known as the Enghien-Cavalry. In 1646, the regiment took the name of the Condé-Cavalry and was ranked 21st rank in its arm. From 1650 to 1665, the regiment was dismantled on several occasions and then reinstated.

In 1757, Condé-Cavalry was placed 20th in rank in its arm. In 1763, Condé-Cavalry was placed 26th in rank being increased from the former Toulouse-Lautrec, created in 1673 to 46th rank. On May 25th 1776, Condé was transferred to the 11th rank in the Dragoons. From 1776 to 1779, the 5th and 6th companies the Légion de Lorraine Chasseurs formed a 5th squadron.

In 1791, the former Condé-Dragoons became the 2nd Dragoons Regiment. *(Page 62)*

12th rank Bourbon Dragoons (prince)

Regiment created on January 17th 1649, for Henri-Jules of Bourbon, son of the Grand Condé, it was named the Enghien- Cavalry. From 1650 and up to 1666, during the *Fronde*, the regiment was dismantled several times and reinstated.

In 1686, the regiment took the name of Bourbon-Cavalry, 22nd rank in its arm and then 21st rank in 1757. In 1763, Bourbon was demoted to the 27th rank and increased from the former Noé created in 1649 to the 32nd rank in the cavalry.

On May 25th 1776, Bourbon was transferred to the 12th rank of the Dragoons. From 1776 to 1779, the 7th and 8th companies from the Légion de Lorraine Chasseurs, formed

(Continued on page 82)

Orléans, 1733-1749

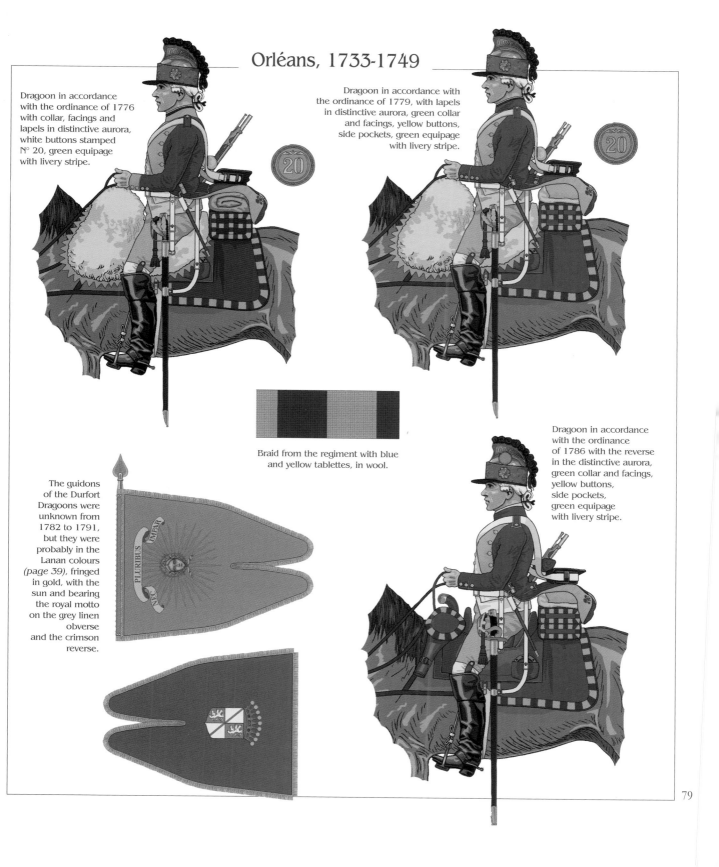

Dragoon in accordance with the ordinance of 1776 with collar, facings and lapels in distinctive aurora, white buttons stamped N° 20, green equipage with livery stripe.

Dragoon in accordance with the ordinance of 1779, with lapels in distinctive aurora, green collar and facings, yellow buttons, side pockets, green equipage with livery stripe.

Braid from the regiment with blue and yellow tablettes, in wool.

The guidons of the Durfort Dragoons were unknown from 1782 to 1791, but they were probably in the Lanan colours *(page 39)*, fringed in gold, with the sun and bearing the royal motto on the grey linen obverse and the crimson reverse.

Dragoon in accordance with the ordinance of 1786 with the reverse in the distinctive aurora, green collar and facings, yellow buttons, side pockets, green equipage with livery stripe.

Dragoon in accordance with the ordinance of 1779, with lapels and facings in distinctive aurora, green collar, white buttons, long pockets, green equipage with livery stripe.

Dragoon in accordance with the ordinance of 1776, with scarlet collar, white facings and lapels, white buttons stamped N° 21, green equipage with livery stripe.

Braid from regiment with white and black tablettes, plain woollen background.

Dragoon in accordance with the ordinance of 1786, with lapels and facings in distinctive aurora, green collar, white buttons, long pockets, green equipage with the livery stripe.

Arms of the Count of Ségur; The regiment of the Ségur Dragoons had the Belsunce guidons *(page 41)*.

Dragoon in surtout with aurora straps, facings without buttons in accordance with the ordinance of 1786.

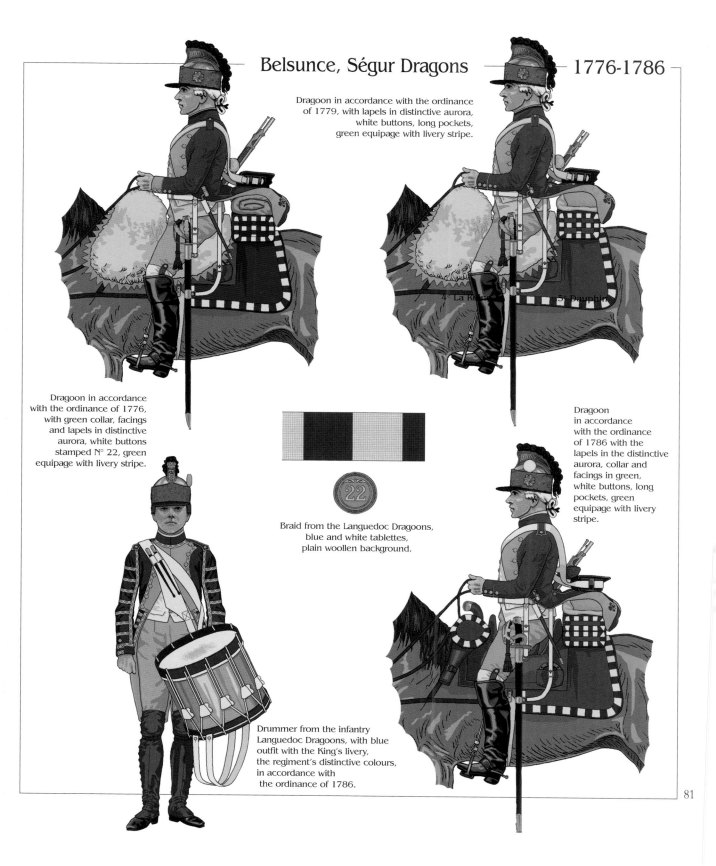

Dragoon in accordance with the ordinance of 1779, with lapels in distinctive aurora, white buttons, long pockets, green equipage with livery stripe.

4° La Reine   5° Dauphin

Dragoon in accordance with the ordinance of 1776, with green collar, facings and lapels in distinctive aurora, white buttons stamped N° 22, green equipage with livery stripe.

Braid from the Languedoc Dragoons, blue and white tablettes, plain woollen background.

Dragoon in accordance with the ordinance of 1786 with the lapels in the distinctive aurora, collar and facings in green, white buttons, long pockets, green equipage with livery stripe.

Drummer from the infantry Languedoc Dragoons, with blue outfit with the King's livery, the regiment's distinctive colours, in accordance with the ordinance of 1786.

a 5th squadron. In 1791, the former Bourbon-Dragoons became the 3rd Dragoon Regiment. *(Pages 63, 65)*

13th rank Conti Dragoons (prince)

Regiment created on July 8th 1667, and placed 15th in the cavalry rank. The regiment used the name of the Marquis de Choiseul-Beaupré in 1667, and then Philippe d'Orléans, Duke of Chartres in 1648.

In 1724 it became the ownership of Louis de Bourbon-Condé, Count of from Clermont, and took the name of the Clermont-Prince-Cavalary, it went down to 22nd rank, and then 23rd rank and in 1762 to 28th rank in the cavalry. In 1771, the regiment became the ownership of Louis-François-Joseph de Bourbon-Conti, Count of La Marche and used the name of the La Marche-Prince Cavalry.

On September 12th 1776, the regiment was transferred to 13th rank in the Dragoons'arm and used the new name of the Conti-Dragoons. From 1776 to 1779, the 1st and 2nd companies from the Légion de Condé Chasseurs formed a 5th squadron.

In 1791, the former Conti-Dragoons became the 4th Dragoon Regiment. *(Page 66)*

14th rank Pinthièvre Dragoons (prince)

Regiment created by Marquis of Heudicourt on March 1st 1674, it was called the Heudicourt-Cavalry and then in 1688 Praslin-Cavalry.

In 1693, it became the ownership of the Count of Toulouse, and then in 1737 his son the Duke of Pinthièvre, it was ranked in 25th place and then 24th in 1757. In 1761, Pinthièvre was increased to the former Escars (created in 1707 to the 58th rank). In 1763, Pinthièvre was reorganised and placed 30th in the cavalry rank.

On March 25th 1776, Pinthièvre was transferred to the 14th rank of the Dragoons. From 1776 to 1779, the 3rd and 4th companies from the Légion de Condé Chasseurs formed a 5th squadron.

In 1791, the former Pinthièvre-Dragoons became the 6th Dragoon Regiment. *(Pages 69,70)*

15th rank Boufflers Dragoons (gentilhomme)

Regiment created on September 24th 1651, under the name of the Humières-Cavalry, placed 22nd in rank and the 24th in 1666. The regiment used the name of its successive Mestres de camp (1675 Seyssac, 1695 Villeroy, 1733 Conti, 1770 Boufflers). In 1757, the regiment was ranked 23rd in its arm and then 29th in 1762. On

March 25th 1776, Boufflers-Cavalry was ranked 15th in the Dragoons arm. From 1776 to 1779, the 5th and 6th companies from the Légion de Condé Chasseurs formed a 5th squadron.

On March 17th 1788, the Boufflers-Dragoons became the 1st rank of chasseurs under the name of the Chasseurs d'Alsace. In 1791, the former Alsace was confirmed as the 1st Regiment from the mounted Chasseurs. *(Page 69)*

16th rank Lorraine Dragoons (prince)

Regiment created in Franche-Comté on September 14th 1673, under the name of the Beauffremont Dragoons, it was ranked 5th in its arm.

In 1690, the regiment was ranked 7th. In 1714, the Balleroy Dragoon Regiment was included into its ranks. In 1733, the regiment was ranked 8th. On May 3rd 1773, the regiment used the name of the House of Lorraine and was ranked 16th.

From 1776 to 1779, the 7th and 8th companies from the Légion de Condé Chasseurs formed a 5th squadron. In 1788, Lorraine was ranked 15th. In 1791, it became the 9th Dragoon Regiment. *(Pages 15, 33, 70, 71)*

17th rank Lescure (gentilhomme)

Regiment created by the Chevalier of Firmaçon, on September 14th 1673, and placed 6th in rank in its arm, it used the name of its successive proprietors (1673 Firmaçon, 1678 Barbezières, 1692 Estrafroms, 1705 Belle-Isle, 1709 Bonnelles, 1727 Arminonville, 1738 Argince, 1742 Surgères, 1745 Aubigné, 1761 Choiseul, 1763 Custine, 1780 Lescure, 1784 Montmorincy).

In 1713, the Vitry Regiment was included into its ranks. In 1776, the regiment was placed 17th in rank. From 1776 to 1779, the 1st and 2nd companies from the Légion de Soubise Chasseurs formed a 5th squadron. On March 9th 1788, the regiment, known as the Chasseurs of Evêchés was ranked 2nd in this arm.

In 1791, the former Chasseurs of Evêchés became the 2nd mounted Chasseurs Regiment. *(Pages 16, 34, 73)*

18th rank La Rochefoucauld Dragoons (gentilhomme)

Regiment created on December 8th 1674, and ranked 8th and then 10th in its arm, it used the names of its successive Mestres de camp and proprietors. (1674 Saint-Sandoux, 1679 Peyssonnel, 1690 Gaubert, 1700 Albert, 1702 Héron, 1705 Bourneuf, 1706 Vassé, 1710 Espinay, 1734 Vibraye, 1745 Caraman, 1761 Autichamp, 1770 La Rochefoucauld,

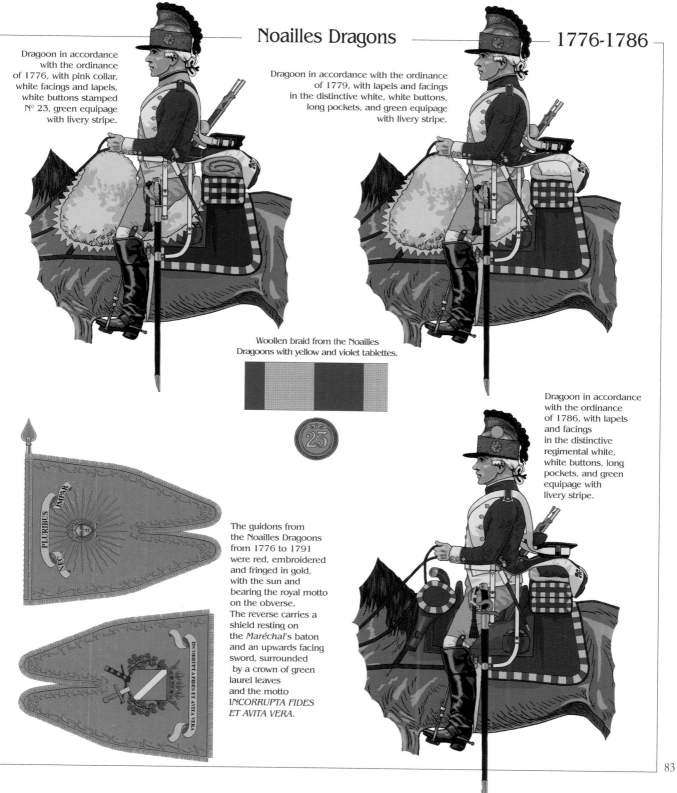

Noailles Dragons

Dragoon in accordance with the ordinance of 1776, with pink collar, white facings and lapels, white buttons stamped N° 23, green equipage with livery stripe.

Dragoon in accordance with the ordinance of 1779, with lapels and facings in the distinctive white, white buttons, long pockets, and green equipage with livery stripe.

Woollen braid from the Noailles Dragoons with yellow and violet tablettes.

Dragoon in accordance with the ordinance of 1786, with lapels and facings in the distinctive regimental white, white buttons, long pockets, and green equipage with livery stripe.

The guidons from the Noailles Dragoons from 1776 to 1791 were red, embroidered and fringed in gold, with the sun and bearing the royal motto on the obverse. The reverse carries a shield resting on the *Maréchal*'s baton and an upwards facing sword, surrounded by a crown of green laurel leaves and the motto *INCORRUPTA FIDES ET AVITA VERA.*

PLURIBUS IMPAR NEC

INCORRUPTA FIDES ET AVITA VERA

1788 Angoulême). In 1713 and 1714, the Guyenne and Espinay regiments were included into its ranks. In 1776, the regiment was placed 18th in rank.

From 1776 to 1779, the 3rd and 4th companies from the Légion of Soubise Chasseurs formed a 5th squadron.

In 1788, the regiment, ranked 16th in its arm, became the ownership of the Duke of Angoulême, and in 1791, it became the 11th Dragoon Regiment. *(Pages 17, 35, 75)*

19th rank Fromux-Ponts Dragoons (gentilhomme)
Regiment created on January 1st 1675, with the Franches

THE REGIMENT IN THE ORDINANCE FROM 1776

All of the squadrons were made up of 60 Dragoons and mounted sub-officers and 40 infantry soldiers, totally 500 men, (300 of whom were on horseback and 200 on foot for each).

The first two squadrons in each regiment were under the command of a
— 1 *Mestre-de-Camp* in second and
— 1 Lieutenant-colonel in second
Each squadron had
— 1 commanding captain
— 1 captain in second
— 1 first lieutenant
— 1 second lieutenant
— 2 sub-lieutenants
— 1 *Maréchal-des-logis* in chief
— 1 second *Maréchal-des-logis*
— 1 Furir-writer,
— 8 brigadiers
— 1 *cadet-gentilhomme*
— 152 Dragoons or chasseurs
— 2 trumpeters
— 1 frater (assistant surgeon)
— 1 farrier

The regiment's headquarters included
— 1 commanding *Mestre-de-camp* (chief of the corps)
— 1 *Mestre-de-camp* in second (second in chief of corps)
— 1 lieutenant-colonel (in charge of administration)
— 1 major
— 1 treasurer quarter master (lieutenant)
— 2 guidon-bearers (*Maréchaux-des-logis* or furirs)
— 1 adjutant (first *Maréchal-des-logis* in chief)
— 1 surgeon-major
— 1 chaplain
— 1 master farrier (*Maréchal-des-logis*)
— 1 master saddler (*Maréchal-des-logis*)
— 1 armourer

companies owned by the Marquis du Fay, and ranked 9th and then in 11th place, it used the name of its successive Mestres de camp (1675 Fay, 1678 La Lanfrom, 1695 Vérac, 1710 Caylus, 1716 Beaucourt, 1725 Vitry, 1739 l'Hôpital, 1749 La Feronnaye, 1762 Chabot, 1770 Jarnac, 1782 Fromux-Ponts).

In 1714, the Rivarole regiment was included into its ranks. In 1776, it was ranked 19th. From 1776 to 1779, the 5th and 6th companies from the Légion de Soubise Chasseurs formed a 5th squadron.

In 1788, the regiment was transformed and took the name of the Chasseurs de Flandres and were ranked 3rd in its arm. In 1791, the former Flandres became the 3rd mounted Casseurs Regiment. *(Pages 18, 36, 77)*

20th rank Durfort Dragoons (gentilhomme)
Regiment created on September 11th 1675, following the amalgam of the former Franches companies, it was placed 11th in rank and then 13th in its arm, it used the name of its successive Mestres de camp (1675 Nancré, 1676 Bursard, 1681 Tessé, 1692 Sinectèrre, 1705 Belabre, 1723 Plélo, 1729 Nicolaï, 1744 Bartillat, 1748 Apchon, 1761 Nicolaï, 1763 Iselin-from-Lanan, 1782 Durfort).

In 1713 and 1714, the Cogneux regiment and part of the Saint-Sernin and Rohan-Chabot regiments were included into its ranks. In 1776, the regiment was ranked 20th. From 1776 to 1779, the 7th and 8th companies from the Légion de Soubise Chasseurs formed a 5th squadron.

In 1788, the regiment was transformed under the name of the Chasseurs of Franche-Comté and was ranked 4th in this arm. In 1791, the former Franche-Comté became the 4th mounted Chasseurs Regiment. *(Pages 20, 39, 79)*

21st rank Ségur Dragoons (gentilhomme)
Regiment created on March 13th 1676, by the House of Asfeld, with the Franche companies of Audigeau, it was ranked 8th and then 14th in the Dragoons, it used the name of its successive Mestres de camp (1676 Asfeld, 1696 Hautefort, 1709 Saumery, 1731 La Suze, 1744 Asfeld, 1749 Thianges, 1761 Chapt-Rastignac, 1764 Belsunce, 1782 Ségur). In 1713 and 1714, the Auzeville and Bozelli regiments were included into its ranks. In 1776, the regiment was ranked 21st.

From 1776 to 1779, the 1st and 2nd companies from the Légion du Dauphiné Chasseurs formed a 5th squadron. In 1788, the regiment was transformed and was renamed the Chasseurs of Hainaut and was ranked 5th in this arm.

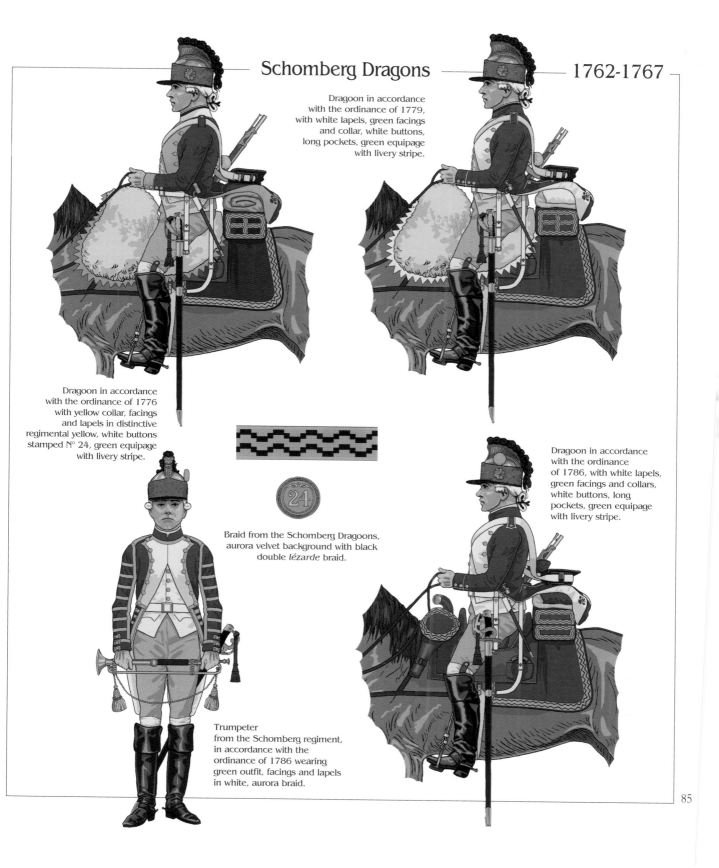

Schomberg Dragons

Dragoon in accordance with the ordinance of 1779, with white lapels, green facings and collar, white buttons, long pockets, green equipage with livery stripe.

Dragoon in accordance with the ordinance of 1776 with yellow collar, facings and lapels in distinctive regimental yellow, white buttons stamped N° 24, green equipage with livery stripe.

Braid from the Schomberg Dragoons, aurora velvet background with black double *lézarde* braid.

Dragoon in accordance with the ordinance of 1786, with white lapels, green facings and collars, white buttons, long pockets, green equipage with livery stripe.

Trumpeter from the Schomberg regiment, in accordance with the ordinance of 1786 wearing green outfit, facings and lapels in white, aurora braid.

85

In 1791, it became the 5th mounted Chasseurs Regiment. (Pages 21, 41, 80)

22nd rank Languedoc Dragoons (gentilhomme)

Regiment created by the Estates of Languedoc on October 4th 1676, and placed 16th in rank in the Dragoons. The regiment kept the name of the province, respecting the will of Louis XIV. In 1713 and 1714, the second regiment of the Languedoc Dragoons, and part of the Bouville Regiment were included into its ranks. In 1776, the regiment was ranked 22nd.

From 1776 to 1779, the 3rd and 4th companies of the Légion du Dauphiné Chasseurs formed a 5th squadron. In 1788, the regiment was transformed and used the name of the Chasseurs du Languedoc and was ranked 6th in this arm. In 1791, it became the 6th mounted Chasseurs Regiment. (Pages 23, 44, 81)

23rd rank Noailles Dragoons (gentilhomme)

Gentilhomme regiment created on December 20th 1688, by the Lieutenant-général Duke of Noailles, it used the name of the Noailles-Cavalry and was ranked 5th in the light cavalry.

In 1754, the regiment used the name of the Ayin-Cavalry (House of Noailles) ranked 54th in the cavalry and then 52nd in 1757.

In 1762, the regiment became the Noailles-Cavalry once again and was placed 31st in rank. In accordance with the ordinance of March 25th 1776, Noailles was transferred to 23rd rank in the Dragoons.

From 1776 to 1779, the 5th and 6th companies of the Légion du Dauphiné Chasseurs formed a 5th squadron. In 1788, the Noailles-Dragoons were placed 17th in rank. In 1791, the former Noailles became the 15th Dragoon Regiment. (Page 64)

24th rank Schomberg Dragoons (gentilhomme)

Regiment created on March 30th 1743, by the Marshal of Saxe, under the name of the Volontaires of Saxe, in 1751 as the Volontaires of Friezin, and then in 1755 as the Volontaires of Schomberg.

In April 1762, the corps became the Schomberg-Dragoons Regiment was ranked 17th in its arm. In 1776, Schomberg was placed 24th in rank. From 1776 to 1779, the 7th and 8th companies from the Légion du Dauphiné Chasseurs formed a 5th squadron.

In 1788, it was ranked 18th in its arm. In 1791, the former Schomberg became the 17th Dragoon Regiment. (Pages 45, 85)

25th rank 1st mounted Chasseurs in 1779

Corps from the Franches Companies created in 1740, under the name of the Volontaires Royaux. On May 7th 1758, the corps had 18 mixed companies, it was called the Légion Royale and was ranked 1st in its arm. In 1776, the légion was disbanded and its mounted companies were transferred to the 1st, 2nd, 3rd and 4th Dragoon regiments. On January 29th 1779, companies were withdrawn from the Dragoon regiments to form the 1st mounted Chasseurs Regiment, and ranked 25th in the Dragoons. In 1784, the regiment used the name of the Chasseurs des Alpes, and then in 1788, the Chasseurs de Picardie, ranked 7th in the mounted Chasseurs arm. In 1791, the former Picardie was conformed as the 7th mounted Chasseurs Regiment.

26th rank 2nd mounted Chasseurs in 1779

Mixed corps created under the name of the Volontaires de Flandre on August 1st 1749, it was comprised of the Arquebusiers de Grassin, the Fusiliers de Morlière, and the Volontaires Bretons. In 1757, the corps transferred half of its troops to form a new corps called the Volontaires de Hainaut. On December 21st 1762, the two corps were assembled with the Volontaires de Dauphiné created in 1760, under the name of the Légion de Flandre, ranked 2nd in its arm. In 1776, the légion was disbanded and its mounted companies were transferred to the 5th, 6th, 7th and 8th Dragoon regiments.

On January 29th 1779, companies were withdrawn from the Dragoon regiments to form the 2nd mounted Chasseurs Regiment, subsequently ranked 26th in the Dragoons. In 1784, the regiment used the name of the Chasseurs des Pyrénées, and then in 1788, the Chasseurs de Guyenne, ranked 8th in its arm. In 1791, the former Guyenne was confirmed as the 8th mounted Chasseurs Regiment.

27th rank 3rd Mounted Chasseurs in 1779

Corps created on April 1st 1757, under the name of the Volontaires de Hainaut. In 1768, the corps used the name of the Légion de Lorraine, 3rd in its arm.

In 1776, the légion was disbanded and its mounted companies were transferred to the 9th, 10th, 11th and 12th Dragoon regiments. On January 29th 1779, companies were withdrawn from the Dragoon regiments to form the 3rd mounted Chasseurs Regiment, ranked 27th in the Dragoons.

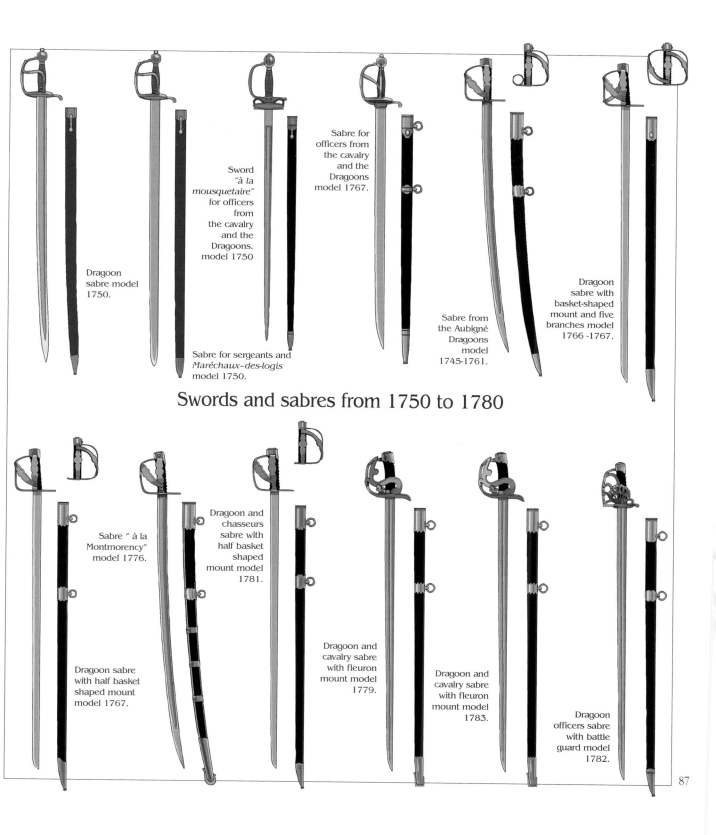

Dragoon sabre model 1750.

Sword *"à la mousquetaire"* for officers from the cavalry and the Dragoons. model 1750

Sabre for sergeants and *Maréchaux–des-logis* model 1750.

Sabre for officers from the cavalry and the Dragoons model 1767.

Sabre from the Aubigné Dragoons model 1745-1761.

Dragoon sabre with basket-shaped mount and five branches model 1766 -1767.

Swords and sabres from 1750 to 1780

Sabre " à la Montmorency" model 1776.

Dragoon sabre with half basket shaped mount model 1767.

Dragoon and chasseurs sabre with half basket shaped mount model 1781.

Dragoon and cavalry sabre with fleuron mount model 1779.

Dragoon and cavalry sabre with fleuron mount model 1783.

Dragoon officers sabre with battle guard model 1782.

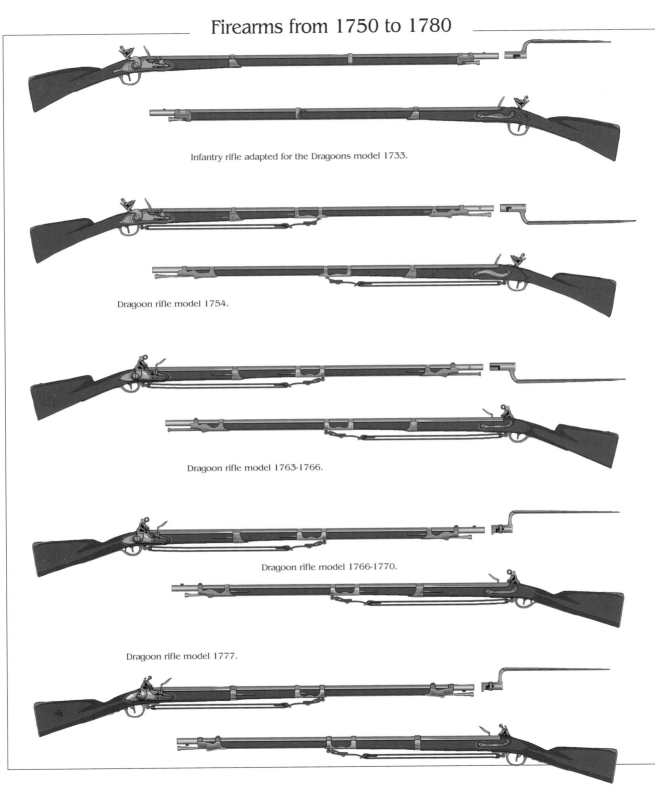

Infantry rifle adapted for the Dragoons model 1733.

Dragoon rifle model 1754.

Dragoon rifle model 1763-1766.

Dragoon rifle model 1766-1770.

Dragoon rifle model 1777.

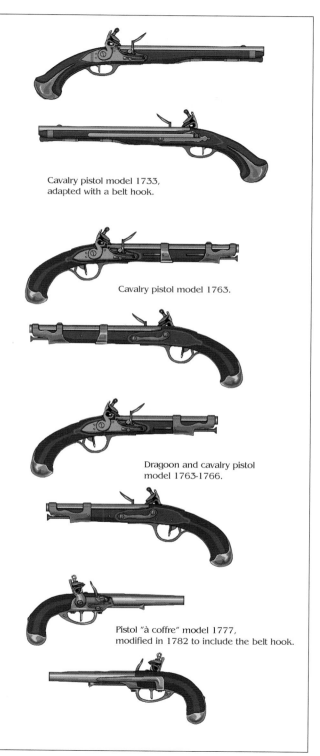

Cavalry pistol model 1733,
adapted with a belt hook.

Cavalry pistol model 1763.

Dragoon and cavalry pistol
model 1763-1766.

Pistol "à coffre" model 1777,
modified in 1782 to include the belt hook.

In 1784, the regiment used the name of the Chasseurs des Vosges and in 1788, the Chasseurs de Lorraine, ranked 9th in the Chasseurs. In 1791, the former Lorraine was confirmed as the 9th mounted Chasseur Regiment.

28th rank 4th mounted Chasseurs in 1779

Corps created on May 7th 1758, under the name of the Volontaires de Clermont-Prince. In 1763, the corps took the title of the Légion Clermont-Prince. In 1766, it was renamed the Légion Condé, ranked 5th in its arm. In 1776, the *légion* was disbanded and its mounted companies were transferred to the 3th, 14th, 15th and 16th Dragoon Regiments. On January 29th 1779, companies were withdrawn from dragoon regiments to form the 4th mounted Chasseur Regiment, ranked 28th in the Dragoons. In 1784, the regiment took the name of the Chasseurs de Cévennes, in 1788 the name of the Chasseurs de Bretagne, ranked 10th in the mounted Chasseurs'arm. In 1791, the former Bretagne was confirmed as the 10th mounted Chasseurs Regiment.

29th rank 5th mounted Chasseurs in 1779

Corps created on January 11th 1762, under the name of the Volontaires Étrangers de Würmser. In 1762, the corps took the name of the Volontaires de Soubise. In 1766, the transformed corps took the title of the Légion Soubise, ranked 6th in its arm. In 1776, the légion was disbanded and its mounted companies were transferred to the 17th, 18th, 19th and 20th Dragoon regiments. On January 29th 1779, companies were withdrawn from the Dragoon regiments to form the 5th mounted Chasseurs Regiment, ranked 29th in the Dragoons. In 1781, the regiment used the name of the Chasseurs de Gévaudan, then in 1788 the Chasseurs de Normandie, ranked 11th in its arm. In 1791, the former Normandie was confirmed as the 11th mounted Chasseurs Regiment.

30th rank 6th mounted Chasseurs in 1779

Corps created on August 10th 1769, under the name of the Légion Corse. In 1775, the corps took the title of the Légion du Dauphiné, it was abolished the following year and its companies were transferred to the 21st, 22nd, 23rd and 24th Dragoon regiments. On January 29th 1779, the corps reformed and was named the Chasseurs des Ardennes, ranked 6th in the chasseurs and 30th in the Dragoons. In 1788, the corps was renamed the Chasseurs de Champagne and placed 11th in rank in the Chasseurs'arm. In 1791, the former Champagne was confirmed as the 12th Mounted Chasseurs Regiment.

Sources and bibliography

ARCHIVES
— *Ordonnance du Roi Concernant les Dragons, from May 1st 1750.*
— *Ordonnance du Roi Concernant les Dragons, from April 9th 1757.*
— *Ordonnance du Roi Concernant les Dragons, from December 21st 1762.*
— *Ordonnance du Roi Concernant les Dragons, from December 25th 1767.*
— *Ordonnance du Roi Concernant les Dragons, from December 21st 1772.*
— *Ordonnance du Roi Concernant les Dragons, from May 31st 1776.*
— *Ordonnance du Roi Concernant les Dragons, from February 21st 1779.*
— *Ordonnance du Roi Concernant les Dragons, from October 21st 1786*
— *État Militaire de France.* From 1758 to 1788.

MEMOIRS AND STUDIES
— Général Pajol, *Les guerres sous Louis XV.* Éditions Firmin-Didot, 1881-1891.

— Général Susane. *Histoire de la cavalerie Française.* Paris, Hetzel, 1874.
— M. Martinet. *Historique de 9ᵉ Dragons.* Éditions Artistiques Militaires, 1888.
— Lienhart & Humbert. *Les uniformes de l'armée Française de 1690 à 1894.* DA éditions, 1989.
— M. Pétard. *Des Sabres & des Epées.* Tome I. Éditions du Canonnier, 1999.
— M. Pétard. *Equipements militaires.*
— C. Ariès, M. Pétard. *Les Armes Blanches Militaires Françaises,* 1966-1990.
— L. & F. Funcken. *L'Uniforme & les armes des soldats de la Guerre en dentelles.* Tome I & II. Éditions Casterman.
— P. Charrié, *Drapeaux & Etendards du Roi.* Éditions Le léopard d'Or, 1989.
— L. Rousselot, *L'Armée Françaises, Dragons.*

MAGAZINES
— *Tradition magazine, La Gazette des Uniformes, La Gazette des Armes, Figurines, Les Carnets de la Sabretache, Le Bivouac, Le Briquet.*

Design and Layout by Ludovic Letrun — Book executed by the Studio " Éditions des Soixante ", supervised by Jean-Marie Mongin for Histoire & Collections
© HISTOIRE & COLLECTIONS 2015

ISBN: 978-2-35250-423-8

Publisher's number: 35250

A BOOK PUBLISHED BY *HISTOIRE & COLLECTIONS*
5, AVENUE DE LA RÉPUBLIQUE
75011 PARIS
Tel: +33 (0) 1 40 21 18 20
Fax: +33 (0) 1 47 00 51 11
www.histoireetcollections.com

This book has been designed, typed, laid-out and processed by *Histoire & Collections* on fully integrated computer equipment.

Color separation: *Studio H&C*
Print by Pulsio,
Bulgaria, European Union,
March 2015